POCKET
GARDENING
GUIDES

ANNUALS
AND
BIENNIALS

❖

DAVID SQUIRE

POCKET
GARDENING
GUIDES

ANNUALS
AND
BIENNIALS

❖

DAVID SQUIRE

Illustrated by Vana Haggerty

WHITECAP BOOKS

Designed and conceived by

THE BRIDGEWATER BOOK COMPANY LTD

———◦◦◦◦———

Art Directed by PETER BRIDGEWATER

Designed by TERRY JEAVONS

Illustrated by VANA HAGGERTY FLS

Managing Editor ANNA CLARKSON

Edited by MARGOT RICHARDSON

CLB 3508

This edition published in 1995 by

WHITECAP BOOKS LTD

1086 West 3rd Street

North Vancouver

B.C.

Canada V7P 3J6

© 1995 CLB Publishing

Godalming, Surrey, U.K.

Printed and bound in Singapore

ISBN 1-55110-238-2

CONTENTS

EMBROIDERY
AND CARPET BEDDING

BEDDING plants first became popular with the use of foliage plants in outdoor borders as early as 1851, when a well-known gardening writer, Thomas Moore, recommended the use of attractive plants such as maize and kale. Today, we still use variegated and coloured forms of these plants. Interestingly, cannas had been used in bedding designs in Germany slightly earlier, encouraging the use of the term 'German beds' for the following few decades. Another writer, Shirley Hibberd, an admirer of Donald Beaton (see below right), also wrote about other attractively leaved plants. During the 1860s, foliage displays were called 'picturesque bedding'.

CARPET BEDDING
Many low-growing subtropical plants were then being introduced

POPULARIZING
BEDDING PLANTS

George Fleming (1809–76) was a great advocate of bedding plants and wrote about them in magazines such as The Cottage Gardener. *He promoted various plants, experimenting in colour harmonies and contrasts, the planting of upright and trailing species in the same design, and the use of height and proportion in flower beds.*

to gardens, and by 1870 were being grown to form carpets of colour. Most were arranged in geometric patterns, but some were planted to form monograms, especially in large estates.

CARPET BEDDING *became popular during the Victorian era and in 1870 a patterned mound was first planted at the Royal Botanic Gardens, Kew.*

IN THE *mid-1800s, many books gave detailed designs for flower beds. Most arrangements were symmetrical and said to be easy to construct and plant.*

The practice of carpeting flower beds spread to botanical, municipal and town gardens. In a few areas, carpet bedding was even used to advertise newspapers! Town names, clocks and commemorative notices were also depicted in flowers and foliage.

A style of raised decorative motifs, lightly clipped to shape, was also developed.

Carpet bedding is still widely practised, especially by park departments in some popular coastal resorts. And this style of planting can inspire a competitive spirit between gardeners.

In domestic gardens, however, half-hardy, summer-flowering bedding plants are used as part of a yearly cycle. Bulbs such as hyacinths and tulips are planted in the autumn (sometimes in combination with biennials). When their display is finished in early summer, tender bedding plants are introduced, then removed in late summer before planting bulbs again.

LAVATERA TRIMESTRIS, *a popular hardy annual, is native to southern Europe.*

SILENE PENDULA, *a compact, hardy annual, is a parent of several superb varieties.*

EXPERIMENTER SUPREME

Donald Beaton (1802–63) is considered to have been the principal advocate of bedding plants of his generation. In continually questioning the use of colours and plants he freed himself from tradition, promoting only the broadest principals and leaving all possible latitude for further experimentation. His ideas were later absorbed by other garden writers.

A typical Beaton planting pattern

Donald Beaton

WHAT ARE
ANNUALS AND BIENNIALS?

❖

THESE are popular garden flowers, used to create colourful displays. They are easily raised from seeds.

• <u>Hardy annuals</u>: These complete their life-cycle in one season. They are sown outdoors in the positions in which they will grow and produce their flowers. With the onset of frosts in autumn, they soon die. They are mostly sown in spring, but some varieties can also be sown in late summer.

• <u>Half-hardy annuals</u>: Like hardy annuals, these also complete their life-cycle within one season. However, they are slightly tender and therefore are raised in gentle warmth in a greenhouse or conservatory in late winter or early spring, and planted outside as soon as all risk of frost has passed. Raising plants in this way gives them a long growing season.

• <u>Biennials</u>: Unlike annuals, these need two seasons in which to complete their growing cycle. In the first year, seeds are sown in early summer. The seedlings are either thinned to give the remaining plants more room, or moved to a nurserybed. In late summer or autumn (or the following spring in cold climates), plants are transferred to their flowering positions, where they bloom and die during the following year.

VARIABLE NATURE

Some plants can be grown in several ways. This is usually influenced by the climate, but can be solely for the convenience of gardeners and their desire to produce fresh plants each year.

HALF-HARDY ANNUALS

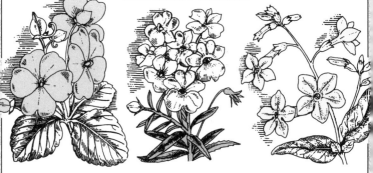

IMPATIENS HYBRIDS
(Busy Lizzie) produce masses of colourful flowers throughout summer. Sow seeds in gentle warmth in late winter or early spring, later planting them in borders. Plants are soon killed by frost in autumn.

NEMESIA STRUMOSA
develops funnel-shaped flowers in compact flower heads during early and mid-summer. Flower colours include yellow, blue, scarlet, orange and bright red. Sow seeds in gentle warmth in late winter or early spring.

NICOTIANA x SANDERAE *creates sweetly-scented flowers in many colours throughout summer. Other Tobacco Plants include N. alata (N. affinis). Like all other half-hardy annuals, seeds are sown in gentle warmth.*

BIENNIALS

ALCEA ROSEA
*(Hollyhock), earlier known
as* Althaea rosea, *is a
perennial but is usually
grown as a biennial. Seeds
are sown outdoors in early
summer and young plants put
into flowering position in late
summer or early autumn.
The flowers appear during
the following summer.*

CAMPANULA MEDIUM
*(Canterbury Bell) develops
masses of bell-shaped flowers
in white, pink, blue or violet
during early and into mid-
summer. Sow seeds in late
spring or early summer and
transplant young plants into
their flowering positions in
autumn, spacing them 25–
30cm/10–12in apart.*

ERYSIMUM x ALLIONII
*(Siberian Wallflower),
earlier known as*
Cheiranthus x allionii,
*produces sweetly scented
flowers during late spring
and into the latter part of
early summer. Sow seeds in
early summer and transfer
plants to their flowering
positions in late summer.*

HARDY ANNUALS

**AMARANTHUS
CAUDATUS** *(Love-lies-
bleeding) is a hardy annual
that develops long, drooping
tassels packed with crimson
flowers from mid-summer to
the frosts of autumn. Seeds
are sown during spring, in
their flowering positions.*

**CALENDULA
OFFICINALIS** *(Pot
Marigold) is well known for
its large, daisy-like flowers in
bright yellow or orange that
appear from late spring to the
frosts of autumn. In spring,
sow seeds where the plants
are to flower.*

IBERIS UMBELLATA
*(Candytuft or Globe
Candytuft) is a hardy annual
that has clusters of white, red
or purple flowers from early
to late summer. Sow seeds in
spring in the position where
the plants are to grow and
develop their flowers.*

PREPARING THE SITE

❖

SINGLE and double digging are the traditional ways in which gardeners cultivate soil in winter. Most soils need only single digging, which entails systematically turning the top 25–27cm/10–11in of soil upside down, at the same time removing perennial weeds and mixing in well-decayed manure or compost.

Double digging is usually only necessary when new gardens are being created. It involves digging soil to the depth of two spade blades, but keeping soil from each level separate. This breaks up the lower depths and enables excess water to drain freely. When dug initially, the surface may appear uneven, especially if the soil has a high clay content, but by spring large clods will have broken down.

Digging in early winter provides a long period for frost, snow, ice and wind to break down the surface, thereby creating a friable tilth for sowing and planting.

Digging is often believed to be tiresome, but if small but increasing amounts are dug at one time, it can become a pleasant exercise. Also, it tidies up the garden.

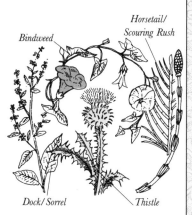

Bindweed

Horsetail/ Scouring Rush

Dock/ Sorrel

Thistle

WHEN *digging soil, always remove perennial weeds. If pieces are left, they re-grow during the following summer and make cultivation difficult. They also rob soil of food and moisture.*

1. DOUBLE *digging is when soil is dug two spits (two spade blades) deep, and the two layers are kept separate. First, take out a trench the depth of a spade's blade and 45–60cm/18–24in wide. Place the soil at one end of the plot, ready for filling the last trench.*

2. USE *a garden fork to dig the lower spit, at the same time mixing in well-decayed manure and compost. This method of cultivating soil breaks up the lower depths, improving drainage and aeration. Roots are also more able to penetrate deeply into the lower soil.*

3. THEN *use a spade to dig out a further 45–60cm/ 18–24in-wide trench, placing the soil on top of the previously forked strip. Continue down the plot in the same way, at the end using soil that was removed from the first trench to fill the last one.*

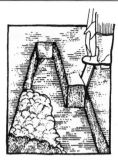

1. SINGLE *digging is when soil is dug one spit deep (the depth of one spade blade). First, dig out a trench one spit deep and 30–38cm/ 12–15in wide across one end of the plot. Then, systematically dig sections of soil and place them upside-down in the trench's base.*

2. EACH *time a new trench is formed, place well-decayed manure or compost evenly along its base. While digging, remove perennial weeds (such as those illustrated on page 10), as well as grubs of soil pests, such as cockchafers, leather-jackets and wireworms.*

3. USE *a spade to form another trench, placing the soil on top of the manure and compost. Continue in this way until the border has been dug. Do not break down large lumps of soil, as frost, snow, rain and wind will accomplish this during late autumn and winter.*

RIDGING SOIL

Although little used today, a form of soil cultivation known as ridging was performed, in past years, when digging clay soil during early winter. It exposed a larger area of soil to frost, winds and snow than normal digging, thereby encouraging a deeper tilth in spring when seeds were sown outdoors. Vegetable beds were the main recipients of this technique, but there is no reason why wide annual borders could not be treated in the same way.

A trench is taken out in the same way as when single digging, but instead of forming a level surface, ridges are formed. After taking out the initial trench, mark the soil into strips three spade blades wide. In each of these strips, dig out and place the first spadeful towards the middle, the second spadeful also towards the middle, and the third one on top. If this is repeated as the border is dug, ridges are formed. In spring use a garden fork or large rake to level the surface.

SOIL CULTIVATION

The need to prepare and cultivate soil has been known for thousands of years. At first, foot ploughs were widely used, while in India and Sri Lanka (Ceylon) buffaloes or bullocks waded through the water in paddy fields to churn up soil earlier softened by flooding.

An inventive but dangerous way to break up hard, impervious subsoil in the tropics and subtropics has been to explode 50g/2oz dynamite charges in holes 75–90cm/ 2½–3ft deep.

Several forms of hand-pushed cultivators have been popular in many countries; a range of fittings to plough, scarify and hoe could be quickly fitted to the framework.

SOWING HARDY ANNUALS

❖

TO ENCOURAGE seeds to germinate, three things are essential: warmth, moisture and air. At this stage neither soil nor compost is needed to initiate germination, but later they are essential to give seedlings stability, nutrition and moisture.

THE RIGHT TIME

It is a waste of time and seeds to try and sow hardy annuals too early in the year, when soil is still cold and wet. In such conditions the seeds will not germinate and may even start to decay due to the excessive moisture that is present. Too much water also prevents air reaching the seeds. The earliest time to sow seeds depends entirely on the climate in your area: even over a distance of one hundred miles further north or south the optimum time may differ by seven to ten days.

Additionally, gardens on south-facing slopes can be sown earlier than north or east-facing ones, while hollows retain moisture and remain cold and inhospitable for several weeks longer than raised areas. Sandy soils are workable earlier than clay types.

Not all seasons have the same temperature and rain pattern. Keep a record each year of the times when you are able to sow hardy annuals, and use this as a general guide. However, if the soil is still wet and cold at that time, do not sow the seeds.

Should the soil not be ready for sowing seeds, do not walk on it as this consolidates the surface unevenly and damages its structure. Also, depressions left by feet, especially on clay soils, may become full of water.

SOIL PREPARATION

Sowing hardy annual seeds begins with the preparation of soil in winter (see pages 10 and 11).

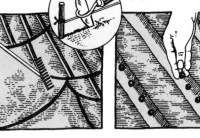
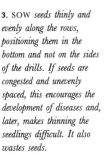

1. AFTER *digging the soil during winter, in spring rake the surface level and systematically tread over the ground, both to firm it and to break down the surface soil to a fine tilth. Shuffle sideways, firming strips no more than 23cm/9in wide at one time. Although time consuming, this task is vital.*

2. RAKE *the soil to obliterate foot prints and to level the surface. Use a pointed stick to mark out the areas for each group of seeds. Then, form shallow drills, 6– 12mm/¼–½in deep, using a draw hoe or the back of an iron rake. Form the drills about 23cm/9in apart – this spacing suits most seeds.*

3. SOW *seeds thinly and evenly along the rows, positioning them in the bottom and not on the sides of the drills. If seeds are congested and unevenly spaced, this encourages the development of diseases and, later, makes thinning the seedlings difficult. It also wastes seeds.*

It is essential that the soil is free from perennial weeds and can be raked to form a horizontal or evenly-sloped surface covered in loose, friable soil. Sowing seeds is featured below; an essential part of this is to shuffle systematically sideways across the plot to consolidate the soil evenly. Do not use a lawn roller as this invariably compacts the soil unevenly when it stops. Also, if the soil is moist it churns up the surface. Using your feet to firm the soil may appear old fashioned and slow, but it is the best way. Afterwards, rake the soil to form an even surface.

THINNING SEEDLINGS

After seeds germinate, the seedlings will need to be thinned to ensure each of them has sufficient space in which to develop. If seedlings are left exactly as they are, many of them will be congested and in immediate competition with their neighbours.

The optimum spacings to which seedlings should be thinned varies from one species to another: these are specified for each of the hardy annuals described in this book.

Preferably, thin seedlings in two stages: first to half the recommended spacing, and later to the full distance. After each thinning operation, re-firm soil around the remaining seedlings to ensure their roots are in close contact with the ground. If left loose, seedlings may die or not develop rapidly. Then, gently water the area.

The seeds are sown in drills about 23cm/9in apart. Therefore, when thinned, the remaining seedlings will not (unless removed to 23cm/9in apart) appear to form squares. Instead, they will form a random pattern. In addition, to keep the display attractive, do not shape the drills so that they are parallel or at right-angles to the front of the border.

DO NOT SOW TOO EARLY

Seeds that are sown too early may rot before they have a chance to germinate. If soil sticks to your shoes when sowing, defer until the surface is dry.

4. COVER *the seeds by using the back of a rake's head and both drawing and pushing friable soil over them. Take care not to push the seeds sideways, so that they are moved out of a straight line, as this may make the removal of weed seedlings from between the rows more difficult.*

5. FIRM *soil over the seeds by using the head of a metal garden rake. It is essential that soil is in close contact with the seeds: this retains moisture around them and ensures the seedlings are firm and secure. Check that the ends of the rows are marked with small sticks, and that the seeds are labelled.*

6. BIRDS *like seeds and can be pests, scratching the soil and scattering them. Traditionally, thin pea-sticks were used to cover the rows until after germination. Alternatively, stretch strong cotton across the bed, about 10cm/4in above the soil, but ensure the birds are not harmed by it.*

SOWING
HALF–HARDY ANNUALS
❖

HALF-HARDY annuals are widely grown for planting in flower beds during summer. They are also planted in tubs, troughs, windowboxes and hanging baskets on patios. These frost-tender plants are raised in gentle warmth in late winter or early spring, pricked out into seed-trays when large enough to handle and slowly accustomed to cooler conditions. When all risk of frost has passed they are planted outdoors.

TEMPERATURES REQUIRED

The warmth needed to encourage germination varies between plants. Temperatures are indicated for each half-hardy annual described in this book. After seeds germinate, lower the temperature slightly to encourage sturdy growth.

The easiest way to provide warmth is to have a heated propagation case. These are warmed by electricity or paraffin. When using an electrically heated unit, ensure its installation has been checked by a competent electrician.

SOWING LARGE SEEDS

Instead of scattering seeds on the compost's surface, large ones are better spaced about 12mm/½in apart. But do not place them closer than 12mm/½in to the sides. Spacing out seeds in this way helps to economize on the number needed and to reduce the risk of congestion and disease.

Good results can be achieved by using an unheated propagation case and placing it on a windowsill indoors. But avoid sunny, south-facing windows as the temperature will be too high and will dry out the compost rapidly. More seeds are killed because the temperature is too high than for any other reason.

1. FILL *a seed-tray with seed compost and gently firm it all over but especially around its edges. Compost that is left loose dries out rapidly and does not encourage the rapid germination of seeds. It also fails to provide a firm base.*

2. ADD *more compost to the seed-tray. To finish the soil's surface, use a straight-edged piece of wood to strike it level with the tray's edges. It may be necessary to pass the wood over the surface several times before it is completely level.*

3. USE *a flat piece of wood (13–15cm/5–6in long, 10cm/4in wide and about 18mm/³⁄4in thick) to firm the compost so that its surface is 12mm/½in below the tray's rim. Nail a small handle to the wood to make it easier to use.*

4. TIP *the seeds into a V-shaped piece of stiff paper and lightly tap its end so that they fall evenly on the surface. Do not sow seeds closer than 12mm/ 1/2in to the edges; if watering is neglected this is where the compost dries first.*

5. USE *a horticultural or domestic sieve to spread compost evenly over the seeds. The depth of the covering varies: some seeds are gently pressed into the surface, while others are covered with 3–6mm/ 1/8–1/4in of finely sieved compost.*

6. WATER *the compost by placing the seed-tray in a bowl filled with 2.5cm/ 1in of water. When moisture seeps to the surface, remove the seed-tray and allow the excess to drain. Do not water from overhead, as this disturbs the seeds.*

THINLY AND EVENLY

There is always a temptation to sow all of the seeds in a seed packet in a single seed-tray, but this is a recipe for disaster. If seeds are congested, each is competing with its neighbour for space, light, air and moisture. They become drawn up, thin and spindly, and never recover. Also, when seedlings are congested there is a greater chance of fungal diseases killing them later.

Large seeds can be spaced apart *(above, left)*, while smaller ones should be encouraged to trickle on to the compost's surface, as illustrated above. Do not sow seeds directly from their packet, as they often then fall in clusters on the compost's surface. If this happens, use the point of a knife to scatter them. Seeds left in the packet can be placed in a screw-top jar in a cool, dark place, but fresh seeds always give the best results.

7. PLACE *a domed, plastic cover over the seed-tray. This helps to maintain a higher temperature, as well as creat-ing humidity and preventing the compost drying. These lids can be bought as a unit with the seed-tray. Always keep clean.*

8. ALTERNATIVELY, *place a piece of glass over the seed-tray. Remove it every day and wipe away condensation. If left, moisture drips on seeds and causes decay. Remember that glass can be hazardous to children and animals if broken.*

9. COVER *the glass or plastic dome with a sheet of newspaper to provide seeds with darkness. Remember to remove it as soon as the seeds germinate. However, a few seeds need light to germinate, so always check the details on the seed packet.*

SOWING BIENNIALS

❖

BIENNIALS take two years to develop flowers. In late spring and early summer of the first year their seeds are sown in well-prepared seed-beds in lightly shaded, sheltered and out-of-the-way parts of gardens. Subsequently, seeds germinate and weeds are removed from between the rows. Later, the young plants are either thinned out or transplanted to a nurserybed.

In late summer or autumn the plants are put into their flowering position in gardens. Occasionally, in very cold areas, this is left until early spring when the soil is workable. Leaving them in a sheltered nurserybed in winter provides them with protection during exceptionally cold weather.

THINNING AND TRANSPLANTING

Sow seeds in rows 23cm/9in apart and 6–12mm/¼–½in deep. The recommended sowing depths for the most popular biennials are given on pages 36 and 37. If the seeds are sown thinly – and the ensuing plants are relatively small – all that is necessary is to thin the seedlings 7.5–10cm/3–4in apart. Daisies *(Bellis perennis)* are an example of this technique. Larger biennials, such as Wallflowers, are thinned 13–15cm/5–6in apart.

However, when seeds are sown close together, the young plants are best forked up as soon as they can be handled and replanted into a nurserybed. Replant them in rows 30cm/12in apart, with 15–23cm/6–9in between them within the rows. When doing this, it is best to water the plants and the nurserybed a few days before transplanting them, as well as afterwards. Commercially, transplanting young biennials is preferred, as it takes less space at the seed-sowing stage.

1. SINGLE *dig a seed-bed in winter to create a weed-free area into which roots can penetrate easily. In mid-spring, rake the soil and slowly shuffle across the bed to consolidate it evenly. Move sideways, firming 23cm/9in-wide strips. This task is absolutely essential.*

2. USE *a rake to level the surface and to remove shoe marks. Rake the soil in several directions to create a deep tilth, but do not bring lumps of soil to the surface. If this happens, remove them completely. A uniform tilth ensures the germination of even seedlings.*

3. INSERT *30cm/12in-long sticks, 23cm/9in apart, along the two opposite sides of the seed-bed. Stretch a garden line between opposite sticks and use a draw hoe to form a V-shaped drill, 6–12mm/¼–½in deep. Ensure that the drill has an even depth.*

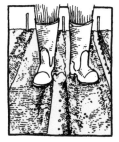

4. SOW *seeds in an even trickle in the drill's base, taking care that they do not fall in clusters. Do not sow seeds direct from the packet; rather, tip a few into your hand and allow them to pass singly between the thumb, index and middle fingers.*

5. COVER *the seeds by straddling the row and slowly shuffling forward. By forming your feet into a V-shape, soil from each side of the drill is pushed inwards to cover the seeds. Alternatively, use the back of a metal rake, but do not disturb the seeds.*

6. FIRM *soil over a drill by covering it with the soles of your shoes, then slowly move sideways. This will consolidate the soil evenly. Another way is to use the top of a metal garden rake to firm the soil while slowly moving along the row.*

PLANTING INTO GARDENS

Planting biennials in late summer and autumn is best, especially when mixing them with bulbs. Clearly, if a flower bed is to be planted solely with biennials, as an edging to a border or between established plants in a border which is a mixture of different plants, the timing is not so critical. But where Wallflowers are to be grown with tulips, for instance, it is best to position both the bulbs and young Wallflowers on the surface before planting them. This enables their positions to be established relative to each other.

The spacings for a range of biennials is detailed on pages 36 and 37, but remember to use the closer distances for short varieties.

Again, water the nurserybed and flower bed before planting them: this will ensure that the plants have the best possible start in life. However, do not make the flower bed so wet that it becomes waterlogged. And lightly water plants when the bed is fully planted. Lastly, make a note of the varieties and their positions, so that judgement can be made later, whether or not to select them again. Keeping a notebook is essential for successful gardening.

SWEET WILLIAMS

At one time these bright-faced, early summer-flowering plants were said to have been named after William the Conqueror, who invaded England from Normandy in 1066. However, a more plausible explanation is that they were named after St. William of Aquitaine. In the 1840s it became a well-known florists' flower, with more than a hundred varieties to choose from.

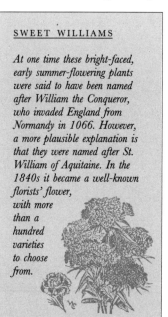

PRICKING OFF
HALF–HARDY ANNUALS

❖

Transferring seedlings of half-hardy annuals from where they were sown is an important operation. If they are left unmoved in the seed-tray in which they were sown, they become congested, weak and spindly, a state from which they never recover. Therefore, as soon as their leaves touch, move them to wider spacings in another seed-tray. This is known as pricking off or pricking out.

SPACING THE SEEDLINGS

In a seed-tray 21.5cm/8½in long and 15cm/6in wide, it is possible to fit twenty seedlings. Do not put the outer ones nearer than 12mm/½in to the sides, as if watering is neglected, it is the tray's edges that dry out first. Commercially, seedlings are set closer together than those suggested here, and this is because more plants can then be raised from the same area. Also, greenhouse space is extremely valuable in spring.

Additionally, by packing in more seedlings it spreads the cost of heating over more plants.

However, for home gardeners with space to spare it makes sense to give each seedling more space in which to develop. And by being more generous with space, seedlings can be left in their seed-tray for a longer period without harming them. This is important, especially when plants have grown large enough to be planted out-doors in spring but the risk of frost prevents this taking place. If the plants were too congested at that stage, they would suffer.

DEPTH OF COMPOST

Most plastic seed-trays are about 5cm/2in deep, but a depth of 6cm/2½in or, preferably, 7.5cm/3in is better as it gives plants a larger reserve of compost if they have to be left in seed-trays while waiting to be planted out. Wooden seed-boxes are usually deeper than plastic types.

1. AS SOON *as seeds germinate, gradually remove the transparent cover so that the seedlings receive plenty of light and air. When their leaves touch, the seedlings must be pricked off so that each seedling has more light, air and space.*

2. WATER *the compost the day before pricking off the seedlings. If the compost is dry, seedlings cannot be successfully transplanted into wider spacings. Use a small fork to lift out a few seedlings and place them on a moist piece of paper.*

3. FILL *a seed-tray with compost and firm it to 12mm/½in below the top. Then, use a small dibber to make holes about 2.5cm/1in deep. Do not position the outside holes nearer than 12mm/½in to the edges of a seed-tray.*

4. TRANSPLANT *each seedling by holding one of its seed leaves and lowering its roots into a hole, so that it is at the same depth as before. While still holding the leaf, very carefully use a dibber to level and firm compost around the roots.*

5. WHEN *the seed-tray is full, gently tap its sides to level loose, uneven compost. (Do not disturb the seedlings.) Then, water the plants from above by using a fine-rosed watering-can. Take care not to disturb the seedlings with the water.*

6. INITIALLY, *place the seed-tray in light shade and gentle warmth. Once the seedlings are established, lower the temperature and place in better light. Keep the compost evenly moist. When their foliage touches, transfer them to pots.*

SELECTING A COMPOST

A hundred years ago, practically every gardening enthusiast had his or her own recipe for successful compost, whether for sowing seeds, pricking off seedlings or potting up plants. About fifty years ago, the John Innes Research Institute standardized composts based on a combination of good topsoil, sharp sand and peat. These are still used today.

But good topsoil has always been difficult to obtain and is variable in composition, so a few decades ago peat-based types were introduced and are now widely used. However, peat is a limited natural resource, and we cannot continue to use it indefinitely. During recent decades, vast areas of peat have been removed. Continually digging up peat not only damages the landscape: it destroys the natural homes of plants, animals and insects.

Environmentally-friendly composts are now being made from coir, bark, wood fibre and straw. Now is the time to convert yourself to friendlier materials.

WHEN PRICKING OFF SEEDLINGS

This is a critical time for seedlings and the first major move in their lives.

• *Ensure the compost they are being put into is clean and free from pests and diseases. Do not use garden soil, as this may contain pests. Reused potting compost may also be infected.*

• *Never move seeds that have dry compost around their roots. Water them the day before and allow excess moisture to drain.*

• *Always hold a seedling by one of its seed leaves, not its stem which is easily bruised and may not recover. Diseases are likely to enter plants with damaged stems. Leaves are hardier, and in any case the seedlings will develop further leaves, but there is only ever one stem.*

• *Never expose newly transplanted seedlings to strong sunlight or high temperatures as these will also damage them.*

POTTING UP
HALF–HARDY ANNUALS
❖

MOST half-hardy annuals are planted into gardens and containers on patios, directly from the seed-trays into which they were pricked off earlier (see pages 18 and 19). However, those that are to be used to brighten homes (see pages 44 and 45) are moved into small pots. A few of these may also need to be repotted subsequently into larger pots.

EXTRA LARGE BEDDING PLANTS
As well as potting up plants for home decoration, various summer-flowering bedding plants such as the Wax Plant (*Begonia semperflorens*) are frequently put into pots to produce extra large plants for garden and container decoration. To create bushy plants, it is essential to grow them in pots: the ends of their shoots are pinched off several times to encourage the development of sideshoots. If these

plants were just left in seed-trays, their foliage would soon become congested. In pots, they can be increasingly spaced further apart.

SINGLE DAHLIAS

Botanically, dahlias are tuberous-rooted perennials from Mexico. In temperate countries they are grown as half-hardy plants: they are unable to survive freezing conditions. As well as being raised by cuttings and division of tubers, there are many brightly coloured, single-flowered forms that can be raised by sowing seeds in gentle warmth in late winter and early spring. Plant them in gardens as soon as the risk of frost has passed.

1. WHEN *the leaves on seedlings (which were earlier pricked off, see pages 18 and 19), touch each other, the young plants should either be planted or moved into small pots. This is known as potting up. If left in trays plants compete for space.*

2. WATER *the plants the day before moving them into small pots. Tap the sides of the seed-tray to loosen the compost, making it easier to remove the plants. Use a small fork to lift a few plants out of the seed-tray. Place them on damp paper.*

3. FILL *the base of a clean pot (about 7.5cm/3in wide) with potting compost and gently firm it. If loam-based compost is used, place a small crock (broken piece of clay pot) in the base. If peat-based compost is used, there is no need to crock the pot.*

ANNUALS AS HOUSEPLANTS

Many plants that are grown as annuals can be displayed indoors as well as in greenhouses and conservatories. A few of the popular ones are featured on pages 44 and 45. These include primulas, Cineraria (Senecio cruentus), Persian Violet (Exacum affine) and Butterfly Flower (Schizanthus pinnatus), also known as Poor Man's Orchid. Some of these grow as perennials in their native countries, but in temperate regions, and as houseplants, are grown as annuals. The Slipper Flower (Calceolaria x herbeohybrida) grows as a biennial: it is sown one year and flowers the next.

Dot plants (see page 62) are also usually potted up, as they are large and dominant.

MAKING MORE SPACE

During spring, in greenhouses, when seeds are being sown, seedlings pricked out and young plants potted up, there is often insufficient space. However, the normal benching can be supplemented by proprietary roof-shelves in aluminium greenhouses, or by suspending wooden planks, about 15–20cm/6–8in wide and 12–18mm/½–¾in thick from wooden glazing bars. Metal coat-hangers can be bent to form trapezes, with their tops hooked over nails or screws.

Double-decker staging is easy to construct by standing planks of wood on large, inverted pots or traditional wooden seed-boxes stood on their sides. If seed-boxes are used, the plank can be nailed to them for extra security.

With all these forms of additional support for seedlings and plants, take care when watering them that excess water does not drip on those below.

4. POSITION *a young plant on compost in the pot's base. The old soil-level mark (indicated by a dark stain on the plant's stem) should be about 12mm/½ in below the pot's rim. Take care not to squeeze or damage the stem, as it may not recover.*

5. FIRM *compost to within 12mm/½ of the rim. It is essential that a space is left at the top of the pot, so that the plant can be watered. If the space is too small, not enough water is given; if too large, there is a risk of over watering.*

6. GENTLY *water the compost by using a fine-rosed watering-can. Allow the excess to drain, then stand the pots close together. As their foliage spreads and grows, space the pots further apart. Keep the compost evenly but not totally moist.*

PLANTING
HALF-HARDY ANNUALS
❖

HESE tender plants are raised in gentle warmth in greenhouses in late winter and early spring. After germination, the seedlings are pricked off and given wider spacings (see pages 18 and 19) and later slowly acclimatized to outdoor conditions.

HALF-HARDY *annuals were traditionally hardened off in English pit lights.*

HARDENING OFF PLANTS
If the plants were raised in a greenhouse, the easiest way to harden them off is initially to lower the temperature slowly and later to leave the ventilators and door fully open, first during the day and then at night.

Traditionally, half-hardy annuals have been hardened off in a garden frame – and this still is an excellent method. Alternatively, place plants on a sunny, sheltered patio during the day and put them in a greenhouse or indoors at night. Later, and if only a light frost is forecast, place several layers of newspaper over the plants. Remove them the following morning, after frost has disappeared.

When seeds have been sown indoors and the plants raised on window sills, increasingly ventilate the area and put the plants outside during the day.

PLANTING
HALF-HARDY ANNUALS
These plants are quickly damaged by frost and therefore must not be planted until all frosts are over. They can bring colour to many places (see right). When planting them, always take out a hole large enough to accommodate the roots. Put the plant in position, spread out its roots and cover with soil or compost, ensuring it is well firmed. Then, lightly water it.

WINDOW SILLS *can be used when acclimatizing half-hardy annuals to outdoor conditions in spring. At night, place them on cool window sills, while during the day put them outside on a warm, sheltered patio.*

GREENHOUSES *are the natural places in which to begin to harden off half-hardy annuals. Slowly increase ventilation during the day. Then, put them outside during the day but back in the greenhouse at night.*

SHELTERED *corners outdoors are ideal when there is little risk of frost, but take care to move the plants inside at night, or to cover with sheets of newspaper if only a light frost is forecast. Remove these when the frost is over.*

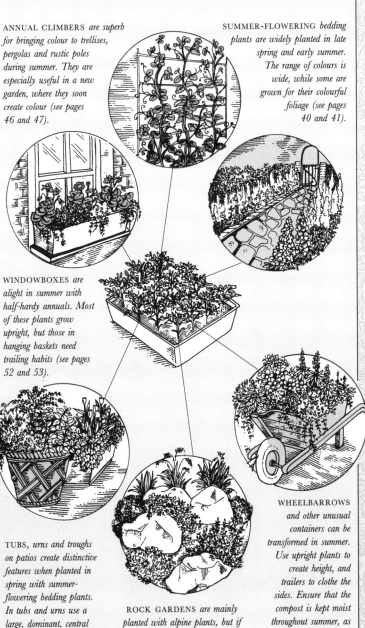

ANNUAL CLIMBERS *are superb for bringing colour to trellises, pergolas and rustic poles during summer. They are especially useful in a new garden, where they soon create colour (see pages 46 and 47).*

SUMMER-FLOWERING *bedding plants are widely planted in late spring and early summer. The range of colours is wide, while some are grown for their colourful foliage (see pages 40 and 41).*

WINDOWBOXES *are alight in summer with half-hardy annuals. Most of these plants grow upright, but those in hanging baskets need trailing habits (see pages 52 and 53).*

TUBS, *urns and troughs on patios create distinctive features when planted in spring with summer-flowering bedding plants. In tubs and urns use a large, dominant, central plant, with trailing types around it so that the container's sides are covered with colour.*

ROCK GARDENS *are mainly planted with alpine plants, but if large – or when newly constructed and not fully planted – small annuals are ideal for introducing 'instant' summer colour (see pages 48 and 49 for suitable plants).*

WHEELBARROWS *and other unusual containers can be transformed in summer. Use upright plants to create height, and trailers to clothe the sides. Ensure that the compost is kept moist throughout summer, as plants soon wilt and die if watering is neglected – even once.*

LOOKING AFTER HARDY ANNUALS

❖

HARDY annuals are easily grown and soon repay the cost of a few packets of seeds, creating a wealth of flowers from early to late summer and sometimes into early autumn. After sowing seeds (see pages 12 and 13), regularly remove weeds from between the rows and the plants. If left, they suffocate the seedlings.

Thinning, supporting and watering seedlings are important tasks, and these are detailed below and on pages 12 and 13. A number of hardy annuals develop into larger plants if sown in late summer, and suitable types are detailed on page 62.

IN AUTUMN

By the onset of autumn, most annuals are past their best and will not be displaying the bright spectacle they did a month or so earlier. Indeed, it is the beginning of autumn frosts that terminate the display; once this has happened, pull up all plants and place them on a compost heap. If they are seriously infested with pests or

DEAD-HEADING PLANTS

Regularly pinching off dead flowers from plants encourages the formation of further blooms. It prolongs the flowering period and reduces the risk of diseases attacking dead flowers and causing healthy ones to become diseased and unsightly.

Some plants, when ageing, cast their petals over the ground, becoming untidy. An example of this is Pot Marigold (Calendula officinalis), *which has large, bright, daisy-like flowers. Cutting off these dead flowers prevents the area becoming an eyesore.*

diseases, burn them. Rake leaves and debris off borders, as they are unsightly and may encourage pests and diseases.

THIN *out hardy annual seedlings as soon as they are large enough to handle. The spaces between them depend on the spread and height of plants (see pages 12 and 13 for details, and pages 30 to 35 for individual spacings).*

MANY *hardy annuals need to be supported. Insert twiggy sticks between young plants, so that stems grow up and through them, eventually forming a canopy of leaves and flowers. If the sticks are too high, trim with secateurs.*

WATER *seedlings and young plants to ensure their roots do not become dry. Use a fine spray to avoid disturbing the soil. Oscillating sprinklers are useful for covering large areas, and can often be controlled by timers.*

LOOKING AFTER BIENNIALS

❖

B IENNIALS are easily grown and create a wealth of colour during their second year. After sowing them in drills in a seed-bed during late spring and early summer of the first year, remove weeds from the seed-bed, water the soil and either thin out the seedlings or transplant them to a nurserybed as soon as they are large enough to be handled.

In late summer or autumn of the same year, established plants can be moved to their flowering positions in gardens. Sometimes, however, when the weather is exceptionally cold or the soil is very wet, they are not moved until spring of the following year.

RE-FIRMING PLANTS

During winter, severe frosts often loosen soil around plants. Therefore, in spring, check each plant and use the heel of a shoe to ensure the soil around it is firm. At the same time, hoe around each plant to break up the crusty surface. This enables air and water to penetrate the soil.

HISTORIC HOLLYHOCKS

Although still widely known as Althaea rosea, *the Hollyhock is properly known as* Alcea rosea. *By nature it is a hardy perennial, but in more temperate climates it is usually grown as a biennial.*

It is thought to be a native of Asia Minor and India and was probably introduced into Europe about the time of the Crusades, during the eleventh to the thirteenth centuries, when it was known as the Holy-hoc. Hoc was the Anglo-Saxon word for mallow. Later, names such as Outlandish Rose *and* Rosa Ultramarina *were accorded it by the Huguenots, the French Protestants who fled their native country during the seventeenth century, many to England.*

PULL *up weeds from between rows of biennial seedlings. If left, they compete with the biennials for light and rob them of moisture and food. They may also harbour pests and diseases. Then, hoe between the rows.*

SOMETIMES, *seedlings are thinned to leave the strongest seedlings (see pages 16 and 17). Alternatively, when large enough to handle, gently fork up young plants and replant into nurserybeds (see pages 16 and 17).*

IN LATE *summer or autumn, transplant young plants into their flowering positions. The distances between plants varies: many biennials are described on pages 36 and 37, with recommendations on spacings.*

HALF-HARDY ANNUALS
Amaranthus – Gazania
❖

BECAUSE all seed-raised plants when growing in their native countries are hardy, the classification 'half-hardy annual' is solely a gardener's term to define plants that when grown in cooler climates need to be raised in gentle warmth. It also enables these plants to be given a longer growing period, which is especially important in cool climates.

RANGE OF
HALF-HARDY ANNUALS
Many plants can be classified in several ways. For example, the Snapdragon (Antirrhinum majus) is native to warm Mediterranean countries, where it persists as a hardy perennial. In temperate regions, however, it is usually grown as a half-hardy annual. It can also be raised as a hardy annual, but in many regions the growing season is so short that it is sown in shallow drills outside in mid to late summer and overwintered outdoors. In mid-spring, plants are transferred to their growing positions.

A further example is the South African Blue Marguerite (Felicia amelloides), a perennial in its native land but grown as a half-hardy annual in temperate regions.

Another advantage of growing plants as half-hardy annuals is that fresh, young, uniform plants are raised at the same time. This enables bedding displays in gardens, as well as in containers on patios, to be planned in detail.

AMARANTHUS HYPOCHONDRIACUS (Prince's Feather) grows 1.2–1.5m/ 4–5ft high and develops deep crimson flower spikes during mid and late summer. Sow seeds 3mm/ 1/8 in deep in 15–16°C/ 59–61°F in early spring. Plant them 75–90cm/ 2½–3ft apart.

ANTIRRHINUM MAJUS (Snapdragon) grows 23cm– 1.2m/ 9–48in high, depending on the variety, and creates flowers from mid-summer to the frosts of autumn. Sow seeds 3mm/ 1/8 in deep in 15–20°C/ 59–68°F in late winter or early spring. Plant them 23–45cm/ 9–18in apart.

ARCTOTIS HYBRIDA (African Daisy) grows 30–60cm/1–2ft high and produces large, brilliantly-coloured, daisy-like flowers throughout summer and until the frosts of autumn. Sow seeds 3–6mm/ 1/8–1/4 in deep in 16–18°C/ 61–64°F in early spring. Plant them 23–38cm/ 9–15cm apart.

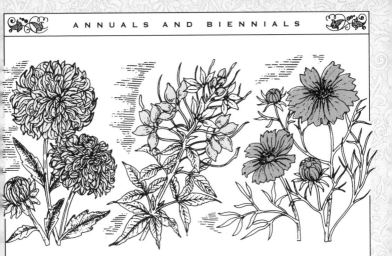

CALLISTEPHUS CHINENSIS *(China Aster)* grows 38–45cm/15–18in high, although there are dwarf forms. They develop petal-packed flowers. Sow seeds 6mm/^{1}/4in deep in 16°C/61°F in early spring. Plant them 23–30cm/9–12in apart.

CLEOME SPINOSA *(Spider Flower/Spider Plant)* grows 90cm–1.2m/3–4ft high and develops large clusters of pinkish, spider-like flowers throughout summer. Sow seeds 3mm/^{1}/8in deep in 18°C/64°F in early spring. Plant them 38–45cm/15–18in apart.

COSMOS BIPINNATUS *(Cosmea/Mexican Aster)* grows 90cm/3ft high and displays white, crimson, pink or rose flowers during mid and late summer. Sow seeds 6mm/^{1}/4in deep in 16°C/61°F in late winter or early spring. Plant them 50–60cm/20–24in apart.

DIDISCUS CAERULEUS *(Blue Lace Flower/Queen Anne's Lace)* is 45–60cm/18–24in high and develops dainty clusters of lavender-blue flowers during mid and late summer. Sow seeds 3mm/^{1}/8in deep in 15°C/59°F during early spring. When planting, space them 23cm/9in apart.

FELICIA AMELLOIDES *(Blue Daisy/Blue Marguerite)* grows about 45cm/18in high and develops sky blue flowers with central yellow discs from early to late summer. Sow seeds 3mm/^{1}/8in deep in 16°C/61°F in late winter or early spring. Plant them 23cm/9in apart.

GAZANIA x HYBRIDA *(Treasure Flower)* grows about 23cm/9in high, with richly coloured, large, daisy-like flowers in shades of orange, yellow, red, pink and ruby from mid-summer to the frosts of autumn. Sow seeds 6mm/^{1}/4in deep in 16°C/61°F in late winter. Plant them 30cm/12in apart.

HALF-HARDY ANNUALS
Heliotropium – Verbena
❖

HELIOTROPIUM x HYBRIDUM *(Cherry Pie/ Heliotrope) grows 30– 45cm/ 12–18in high and produces dark violet, lavender or white flowers throughout summer. Sow seeds 6mm/ ¹/4in deep in 16–18°C/ 61–64°F during late winter. Plant them 30–38cm/ 12–15in apart.*

NICOTIANA ALATA *(Flowering Tobacco Plant) grows 60–90cm/ 2–3ft high and with clusters of tubular, fragrant flowers in a range of colours from early to late summer. Sow seeds 3mm/ ¹/8in deep in 16°C/ 61°F during late winter and early spring. Plant them 23– 30cm/ 9–12in apart.*

LOBELIA ERINUS *(Edging Lobelia) grows 10–23cm/ 4–9in high; but some varieties are trailing. Mainly in blue, white or red from early summer to autumn. frosts. Sow thinly on compost surface during late winter or early spring and place in 16°C/ 61°F. Plant them about 10cm/ 4in apart.*

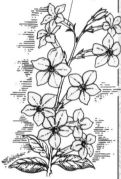

IMPATIENS WALLERIANA *(Busy Lizzie) grows 45– 60cm/ 1¹/2–2ft high and flowers profusely all summer. Sow seeds 3mm/ ¹/8in deep in 16°C/ 61°F in early spring. Plant them 23–30cm/ 9–12in apart.*

FURTHER HALF-HARDY ANNUALS

- Ageratum houstonianum *(Floss Flower/ Pussy-foot)* − page 38.
- Alonsoa warscewiczii *(Mask Flower).*
- Alyssum maritimum/Lobularia maritima *(Sweet Alyssum)* − page 50.
- Begonia semperflorens *(Wax Plant)* − page 38.
- Cotula barbata *(Pincushion Flower).*
- Emilia flammea *(Tassel Flower).*
- Felicia bergeriana *(Kingfisher Daisy)* − page 48.
- Gaillardia pulchella *(Blanket Flower)* − page 55.
- Mimulus *(Monkey Flower).*
- Nemesia strumosa − *page 43.*
- Salpiglossis sinuata *(Painted Tongue).*
- Tagetes erecta *(African Marigold).*
- Ursinia anethoides − *page 49.*

PETUNIA x HYBRIDA
*grows 15–38cm/ 6–15in
high, with trumpet-shaped
flowers in many colours
throughout summer. Lightly
press seeds on the surface of
compost in late winter or
early spring and place in
16°C/ 61°F. Plant
15–30cm/ 6–12in apart.*

SALVIA SPLENDENS
*(Scarlet Salvia) grows
30–38cm/ 12–15in high
and creates a mass of scarlet
flowers from mid-summer to
the frosts of autumn. There
are also white, purple and
salmon varieties. Sow seeds
6mm/ 1/4in deep in 16°C/
61°F in late winter or early
summer. Plant 23–38cm/
9–15in apart.*

TAGETES PATULA
*(French Marigold) grows
15–30cm/ 6–12in high and
develops yellow or mahogany-
red, daisy-like flowers
throughout summer. There
are both single and double-
flowered forms. Sow seeds
6mm/ 1/4in deep in 16°C/
61°F during late winter or
early spring. Plant them
15–30cm/ 6–12in apart.*

PHLOX DRUMMONDII
*(Annual Phlox) grows about
38cm/ 15in high and
develops dense heads of pink,
purple, red, lavender and
white flowers from mid to
late summer. Sow seeds
6mm/ 1/4in deep in late
winter or early spring and
place in 15°C/ 59°F. Plant
them 23cm/ 9in apart. Also
dwarf forms, 15–23cm/
6–9in high.*

VERBENA x HYBRIDA
*(Vervain) grows 15–38cm/
6–15in high and from early
summer to the frosts of
autumn produces bright,
dome-shaped heads of scarlet,
carmine, blue and white
flowers, set against dark
serrated leaves. Sow seeds
3mm/ 1/8in deep in
16°C/ 61°F in late winter
or early spring. Plant them
15–25cm/ 6–10in apart.*

HARDY ANNUALS
Amaranthus – Clarkia
❖

THESE are plants that can be sown outside in the positions in which they will flower. Sometimes, seeds are scattered on the soil's surface and lightly raked in. But it is much better to form drills about 23cm/9in apart.

Sowing seeds in drills enables weeds between the rows to be identified and removed while still small. Sow seeds thinly and evenly, and after germination thin the seedlings to the distances indicated on this and other pages.

Hardy annuals are ideal plants for children to sow, as they soon create a vibrant display which usually continues throughout summer. Most hardy annuals germinate within two to four weeks, although much depends on the moisture in the soil and its temperature: cold, wet soil delays the germination of seeds. The local climate also has a strong influence on germination.

HARDY VARIATIONS

As with half-hardy annuals, many hardy types have a different nature in their native countries. *Anchusa capensis*, for example, is a biennial in its native South Africa, but in temperate regions is better grown as a hardy annual. The well-known Black-eyed Susan *(Rudbeckia hirta)* is a short-lived perennial from North America and usually grown as a hardy annual. It can also be raised as a half-hardy annual, especially where the growing season is short.

BORAGO OFFICINALIS
(Borage/Tailwort) is a well-known herb with blue, star-shaped, pendent flowers throughout summer. It grows 45–75cm/1¹/2–2¹/2ft high. Sow seeds 6–12mm/¹/4–¹/2in deep in drills 23cm/9in apart during mid-spring. Thin the seedlings 30cm/12in apart.

ANCHUSA CAPENSIS
grows about 45cm/18in high and develops blue, saucer-shaped flowers in dense terminal clusters from mid to late summer. Sow seeds 6–12mm/¹/4–¹/2in deep in drills 23cm/9in apart during spring. Later, thin the seedlings 15–23mm/6–9in apart.

CALENDULA OFFICINALIS *(Pot Marigold) grows 30–60cm/1–2ft high, and from late spring to autumn produces large, bright yellow or orange flowers. Sow seeds 12mm/¹/2in deep in drills 23cm/9in apart during spring. Thin the seedlings 30cm/12in apart.*

CENTAUREA CYANUS *(Cornflower) grows 23–90cm/9–36in high and develops masses of pink, red, purple, blue or white, button-like flowers throughout summer. Sow seeds 12mm/^{1}/$_2$in deep in drills 23–30cm/9–12in apart during spring. Thin the seedlings 23–38cm/9–15in apart.*

CENTAUREA MOSCHATA *(Sweet Sultan) grows 50–60cm/20–24in high and produces white, yellow, pink or purple, cornflower-like flowers from early to late summer. Sow seeds 6mm/^{1}/$_4$in deep in drills 23cm/9in apart in spring. Subsequently, thin the seedlings 23cm/9in apart.*

CHRYSANTHEMUM CARINATUM *(Tricolor Chrysanthemum and often known as* C. tricolor) *grows 50–60cm/20–24in high with flowers about 6cm/2^1/$_2$in wide in summer. Sow seeds in spring 6mm/^{1}/$_4$in deep in drills 23cm/9in apart. Thin to 15–23cm/6–9in apart.*

CLARKIA PULCHELLA *grows about 45cm/18in high and develops dainty sprays of white, rose or violet flowers from mid to late summer. Sow seeds 6mm/^{1}/$_4$in deep in drills 23cm/9in apart during spring and early summer. Thin the seedlings 25–30cm/10–12in apart. Native to North America, it has a branching and delicate nature with mid-green leaves.*

CLARKIA ELEGANS *grows 60cm/2ft high and from early to late summer develops white, lavender, salmon-pink, orange, purple or scarlet flowers. Sow seeds 6mm/^{1}/$_4$in deep in drills 23cm/9in apart during spring and early summer. Subsequently, thin seedlings 25–30cm/10–12in apart.*

A WEED IN CORNFIELDS

*The pretty, blue Cornflower (*Centaurea cyanus) *used to be a troublesome weed in crops, but better threshing and improved seed technology has almost eliminated it. In years gone by, it was used in garlands, while in Saxony the flowers were boiled and added to beer to cure jaundice.*

HARDY ANNUALS
Echium – Linaria
❖

ECHIUM LYCOPSIS *(Viper's Bugloss)* grows 75–90cm/ 2¹/₂ –3ft tall, but it is the 30cm/12in-high garden hybrids that are mainly grown. Sow seeds 6mm/ ¹/₄ in deep in spring and thin the seedlings 23–30cm/ 9–12in apart.

GILIA LUTEA *(Stardust)* grows 10–15cm/ 4–6in high and develops star-shaped, brightly-coloured flowers in yellow, orange, red and pink from early to late summer. Sow seeds 6mm/ ¹/₄ in deep in drills 23cm/ 9in apart during spring. Thin the seedlings 10cm/ 4in apart.

EUPHORBIA MARGINATA *(Snow on the Mountain)* grows about 60cm/ 2ft high, with soft green leaves veined and edged in white. Insignificant white flowers appear in late summer. Sow seeds 6mm/ ¹/₄ in deep in drills 23cm/ 9in apart during spring. Thin the seedlings 25–30cm/ 10–12in apart.

ESCHSCHOLZIA CALIFORNICA *(Californian Poppy)* grows 30–38cm/ 12–15in high and creates a wealth of rose, yellow, orange, white and red flowers throughout summer. Sow seeds 6mm/ ¹/₄ in deep in drills 23cm/ 9in apart during mid-spring. Thin to 23–30cm/ 9–12in apart.

LAND OF FIRE

In its native California, the Californian Poppy (Eschscholtzia californica) *was at one time so prolific that Spanish settlers named the country* The Land of Fire *and* The Golden West. *The flowers are said to have a soporific effect, and the leaves have been used as food by the local Native Americans.*

Californian Poppy

ANCIENT PLANT

Candytuft gained its name from its native country, Candia, an earlier name for Crete. By the sixteenth century it was known as Candy Thlaspie, while a couple of centuries later it became Candy-turf.
During the first century after the birth of Christ, the Greeks were using its seeds as mustard with meat.

LAVATERA TRIMESTRIS *(Mallow) forms a bushy plant 60–90cm/2–3ft high with large, bell-shaped, rosy-pink, satin-like flowers from mid to late summer. Sow seeds 12mm/^{1}/2in deep in drills 23cm/9in apart in mid to late spring. Thin the seedlings 45–50cm/18–20in apart.*

HELIANTHUS ANNUUS *(Sunflower/Mirasol) grows 90cm–3m/3–10ft high and has large flowers from mid to late summer. Sow seeds 12mm/^{1}/2in deep in drills 30–38cm/12–15in apart in late spring. Thin to 30–45cm/12–18in apart.*

HIBISCUS TRIONUM *(Flower-of-an-Hour) grows about 38cm/15in high and creates primrose-coloured flowers with maroon eyes throughout summer. Sow seeds 6mm/^{1}/4in deep in drills 23cm/9in apart during spring. Thin the seedlings 25–30cm/10–12in apart.*

LINARIA MAROCCANA *(Toadflax/Fairy Flax) grows 20–38cm/8–15in high with flowers in pink, red, yellow, violet and blue during early and mid-summer. Sow seeds 3mm/^{1}/8–^{1}/4in deep in drills 15–23cm/6–9in apart during spring. Thin to 15cm/6in apart.*

IBERIS UMBELLATA *(Candytuft/Globe Candytuft) grows 15–38cm/6–15in high and develops domed heads of white, red or purple flowers from early to late summer. Sow seeds 6mm/^{1}/4in deep in drills 23cm/9in apart during early and mid-spring. Later, thin the seedlings 23cm/9in apart.*

HARDY ANNUALS
Linum – Scabiosa
❖

LINUM GRANDIFLORUM 'RUBRUM' *(Scarlet Flax) grows 30cm/12in high and develops saucer-shaped, brilliant crimson flowers on slender stems from early to late summer. Sow seeds 6mm/1/4in deep in drills 23cm/9in apart in spring. Subsequently, thin the seedlings 13–15cm 5–6in apart.*

MALCOLMIA MARITIMA *(Virginian Stock) is 20–30cm/8–12in high and throughout summer develops red, lilac, rose or white flowers, each lasting about four weeks. For a constant display, sow seeds 6mm/ 1/4in deep every few weeks from spring to mid-summer, in drills 23cm/9in apart. Later, thin the seedlings to about 13cm/5in apart.*

MENTZELIA LINDLEYI *grows about 45cm/18in high, with golden yellow, sweetly scented flowers from early to mid-summer. Sow seeds 6mm/1/4in deep in drills 23cm/9in apart during spring. Subsequently, thin the seedlings to about 23cm/9in apart.*

SUN GOD EMBLEM

*The well-known Sunflower (*Helianthus annuus*) is native to Central America and Peru, where its likeness was carved on Inca temples as an emblem of the Sun God. It was also cast in gold and worn by virgins of the sun, and priests. Nowadays, it is commonly associated with the late nineteenth century Dutch painter, Vincent Van Gogh. The plant is increasingly grown for its seeds, from which sunflower oil is extracted, while before the development of synthetic dyes the flowers were a valuable source of yellow dye.*

NIGELLA DAMASCENA *(Love-in-a-mist) grows 45–60cm/1 1/2–2ft high, with blue or white flowers from early to mid-summer. Sow seeds 6mm/1/4in deep in drills 23cm/9in apart during spring. Thin the seedlings 15–23cm/6–9in apart.*

PAPAVER RHOEAS (Field Poppy) grows 50–60cm/ 20–24in high, with red, black–centred, 7.5cm/3in-wide flowers from early to mid-summer. Sow seeds 6mm/¹/₄in deep in drills 23cm/9in apart during spring. Thin the seedlings 25–30cm/10–12in apart.

FURTHER HARDY ANNUALS

- Adonis aestivalis (Pheasant's Eye) – page 48.
- Asperula orientalis (Annual Woodruff).
- Coreopsis drummondii.
- Coreopsis tinctoria (Calliopsis).
- Cynoglossum Amabile (Hound's Tongue).
- Delphinium consolida (Larkspur) – page 54.
- Gypsophila elegans (Baby's Breath) – page 55.
- Ionopsidium acaule (Violet Cress) – page 49.
- Lathyrus odoratus (Sweet Pea).
- Limnanthes douglasii (Poached Egg Plant) – page 49.
- Malcolmia maritima (Virginian Stock – page 51.
- Matthiola bicornis (Night–scented Stock).
- Nemophila menziesii (Baby Blue Eyes) – page 39.
- Reseda odorata (Mignonette) – page 51.

PAPAVER SOMNIFERUM (Opium Poppy) grows 75cm/2¹/₂ft high and from early to mid-summer produces white, pink, scarlet or purple flowers, followed by the well-known, bulbous seed-heads. Sow seeds 6mm/¹/₄in apart during spring. Thin the seedlings 30cm/12in apart.

RUDBECKIA HIRTA (Black-eyed Susan), when grown as a hardy annual, is 30–90cm/1–3ft high and develops golden yellow flowers during mid and late summer. Sow seeds 6mm/ ¹/₄in deep in drills 23cm/ 9in apart, in spring. Thin the seedlings 30–45cm/ 12–18in apart.

SCABIOSA ATROPURPUREA (Sweet Scabious) grows 90cm/3ft high, but dwarf types are only 38–45cm/15–18in high. Blooms in many shades from mid to late summer. Sow seeds 12mm/¹/₂in deep in drills 23cm/9in apart during spring. Thin the seedlings 23cm/9in apart.

BEAUTIFUL BIENNIALS

❖

THESE are plants that are sown during one year, germinate and establish themselves as plants, and then develop flowers during the following season. They are hardy and able to survive outdoors during winter. Most of them flower in late spring and early summer, while a few continue in bloom throughout the summer.

Many, such as Hollyhocks *(Alcea rosea)*, Daisies *(Bellis perennis)* and Wallflowers *(Cheiranthus* and *Erysimum)* are hardy perennials that are normally grown as biennials. This enables a large number of plants to be raised at one time, so that a concentrated display can be created in gardens. Some are grown in flower beds in association with bulbs.

Foxgloves *(Digitalis purpurea)* and Forget-me-nots are both grow naturally as biennials.

FURTHER BIENNIALS

- *Aquilega* x *vulgaris* (Granny's Bonnet/Columbine).
- *Erysimum alpinum* (Alpine Wallflower/Fairy Wallflower).
- *Lunaria annua* (Honesty, and earlier known by the name of *Lunaria biennis*).
- *Lunaria annua 'Variegata'* (Variegated Honesty).

Sowing and raising biennials is detailed on pages 16 and 17, and looking after them on page 25. These pages include the depths at which seeds are sown.

After being thinned out, they are put into their flowering positions mainly in late summer or autumn, and sometimes in spring.

ALCEA ROSEA
(Hollyhock) grows about 1.8m/6ft high. Sow seeds 12mm/^{1}/2 in deep in rows 23cm/9in apart in a seed-bed in early or mid-summer. In late summer, move young plants to their flowering positions, setting them 60cm/2ft apart.

BELLIS PERENNIS
(Daisy) grows 10–15cm/ 4–6in high, and from spring to late summer produces white, pink or red flowers. Sow seeds 6mm/^{1}/4 in deep in early summer. In late summer, move them to their flowering positions, about 13cm/5in apart.

CAMPANULA MEDIUM
(Canterbury Bell) grows 38–90cm/15–36in high, with white, pink, blue or violet flowers during early and mid-summer. Sow seeds 6mm/^{1}/4 in deep in a seed-bed in early summer. In autumn, plant them 25– 30cm/10–12in apart.

ERYSIMUM x ALLIONII
*(Siberian Wallflower), also
known as* Cheiranthus x
allionii, *grows 38cm/15in
high. In late spring and early
summer it displays orange
flowers. Sow seeds 6mm/
^{1}/4in deep in a seed-bed in
early summer. Put plants
into their flowering positions
in late summer, setting them
25–30cm/10–12in apart.*

CHEIRANTHUS CHEIRI
*(Wallflower) grows 20–
60cm/8–24in high and
develops mainly red, yellow
or orange flowers during late
spring and early summer.
Sow seeds 6mm/^{1}/4in deep
in a seed-bed in early
summer; in late summer,
plant dwarf varieties 25cm/
10in apart, tall ones
30–38cm/12–15in.*

DIANTHUS BARBATUS
*(Sweet William) grows
30–60cm/12–24in high
and develops dense heads of
flowers during early and
mid-summer. Sow seeds
6mm/^{1}/4in deep in a seed-
bed in early summer. Move
plants to their flowering
positions in late summer,
setting them 20–25cm/
8–10in apart.*

DIGITALIS PURPUREA
*(Foxglove) grows 90cm–
1.5m/3–5ft high. Spires of
bell-shaped flowers develop in
early and mid-summer. Sow
seeds shallowly in late spring,
then set plants 15cm/6in
apart in a nurserybed. In
late summer plant out 45–
60cm/1^1/2–2ft apart.*

MYOSOTIS ALPESTRIS
*(Forget-me-not) grows
10–20cm/4–8in high, and
during late spring and early
summer creates masses of
blue flowers. Sow seeds
6mm/^{1}/4in deep in a seed-
bed during early summer. In
late summer, plant them
15cm/6in apart.*

**VIOLA x
WITTROCKIANA**
*15–23cm/6–9in high,
normally flowers in late
spring and early summer
(also summer and winter
types). Sow seeds 6mm/
^{1}/4in deep in early summer.
In late summer, plant them
out, about 23cm/9in apart.*

ANNUALS AND BIENNIALS FOR PARTIAL SHADE

❖

NO PLANT will thrive in deep shade, but here are a few annuals and biennials that will survive partial or light shade. They are more tolerant of these positions if the soil is slightly moist: dry soil is a strain on plants and can soon cause their deaths when combined with deep shade.

Plants in these positions will not be as large or as floriferous as those in ideal conditions where light and moisture are readily available. Therefore, in shady areas plant them slightly closer together or thin the seedlings to smaller spacings.

If the area is moist as well as shady, slugs and snails will be more of a problem. Therefore remember to check all the plants regularly, especially in early summer when nights become warmer.

CANTERBURY OR COVENTRY BELLS?

During the sixteenth and seventeenth centuries, Campanula medium *(now widely known as Canterbury Bell) was called Coventry Bells. The name Canterbury Bells was then being used for* Campanula trachelium, *now known as Throatwort (from its use as a gargle) or Bats-in-the-Belfry. The flowers of Throatwort resembled the metal St. Thomas bells which were sold as badges to pilgrims visiting the shrine of St. Thomas à Becket in Canterbury Cathedral. The bells were often used by pilgrims to adorn their horses.*

ASPERULA ORIENTALIS *(Annual Woodruff) is a hardy annual, growing 30cm/12in high, with pale blue flowers during mid-summer. Sow seeds in spring or early summer, 6mm/¹/4 in deep in drills 23cm/9in apart. Thin the seedlings 10cm/4in apart.*

AGERATUM HOUSTONIANUM *(Floss Flower) is a half-hardy annual, 13–30cm/5–12in high and with bluish-mauve flowers throughout summer. Sow seeds 3mm/¹/8 in deep in late winter and place in 16–18°C/61–64°F. Later, plant them 15–25cm/6–10in apart.*

BEGONIA SEMPERFLORENS *(Wax plant) is a half-hardy annual, 15–23cm/6–9in high, with flowers throughout summer. Sow seeds thinly on the compost surface in late winter, place in 18°C/64°F and prick out the seedlings in small clusters. Later, plant 15–23cm/6–9in apart.*

BIENNIALS FOR LIGHT SHADE

- Aquilegia vulgaris *(Granny's Bonnet/ Columbine)*.
- Bellis perennis *(Daisy)*.
- Campanula medium *(Canterbury Bell)*.
- Digitalis purpurea *(Foxglove)*.
- Myosotis *(Forget-me-not)*.

LINUM GRANDIFLORUM *(Flax) is a hardy annual 38–45cm/ 15–18in high and with rose-coloured flowers from early to mid-summer. Sow seeds 6mm/ 1/4in deep in drills 23cm/ 9in apart during spring, in their flowering positions. Thin the seedlings 13cm/ 5in apart.*

COLLINSIA HETEROPHYLLA *(Chinese Houses) is a hardy annual, 60cm/ 2ft high, with bright flowers from early to late summer. Sow seeds 6mm/ 1/4in deep in drills 23cm/ 9in apart during late spring, where the plants are to flower. Thin the seedlings 15cm/ 6in apart.*

HESPERIS MATRONALIS *(Damask Violet/ Sweet Rocket) is a short-lived perennial usually grown as a biennial, flowering in early summer. Sow seeds 6mm/ 1/4in deep in a seed-bed in early summer. Move young plants into a nurserybed and plant into a border in late summer or autumn. Set the plants 38–45cm/ 15–18in apart.*

NEMOPHILA MENZIESII *(Baby Blue Eyes and also known as* N. insignis*) is a hardy annual growing 23cm/ 9in high and with sky blue, saucer-shaped flowers from early to mid-summer. Sow seeds 6mm/ 1/4in deep in drills 23cm/ 9in apart in spring, where the plants are to flower. Thin the seedlings 15cm/ 6in apart.*

COREOPSIS TINCTORIA *(Calliopsis and also known as* C. bicolor*) is a hardy annual, 23–75cm/ 9–30in high and with golden yellow, maroon or crimson flowers from mid to late summer. Sow seeds 6mm/ 1/4in deep in drills 23cm/ 9in apart in spring, where they are to flower. Subsequently, thin the seedlings 15–30cm/ 6–12in apart.*

COLOURED AND VARIEGATED FOLIAGE

❖

COLOURFUL leaves of foliage plants introduce brightness and permanency throughout summer. Some of these plants can be sown where they are to flower, others in gentle warmth in spring, while a few are biennials.

Many of these plants have bright and strong colours, so use them carefully to ensure they do not dominate other plants. Some, such as *Atriplex hortensis cupreata*, can be used to create attractive backgrounds for other plants. *Kochia scoparia* 'Trichophylla', however, is ideal for creating height variations in borders. Ornamental cabbages form unusual banks of colour and are available in a wide range of shades. Some are 38cm/ 15in or more across, with attractively frilled edges to their leaves.

AMARANTHUS TRICOLOR (Joseph's Coat) is a half-hardy annual that grows 60–90cm/ 2–3ft high and has a mass of green leaves that are variegated with crimson or scarlet, and are beautifully overlaid with yellow and bronze.

BRASSICA 'ROSE BOUQUET' (Ornamental Cabbage) is best grown as a half-hardy annual. This variety has reddish-pink leaves, but there is a variety of others. Their colours are enhanced by autumn frosts.

ATRIPLEX HORTENSIS CUPREATA (Red Mountain Spinach/ Red Orach) is a hardy annual, about 1.2m/ 4ft high with beetroot-red foliage throughout summer. It is ideal as a dominantly coloured background for other plants.

COLEUS BLUMEI (Flame Nettle) is a tender greenhouse plant which, during summer, is ideal for planting in containers on a patio. Some varieties are superb in hanging baskets. The nettle-like leaves are vibrantly coloured with a range of bright, eye-catching shades.

EUPHORBIA MARGINATA *'Summer Icicle'* is a hardy annual about 45cm/18in high. The white leaves have green centres. It can also be raised as a half-hardy annual.

PERILLA FRUTESCENS *'Nankinensis'* is a half-hardy annual with bronze-purple, finely cut leaves. It grows about 60cm/2ft high.

KOCHIA SCOPARIA *'Trichophylla'* (Summer Cypress/Burning Bush) is grown as a half-hardy annual, 60–90cm/2–3ft high.

RICINUS COMMUNIS *'Carmencita'* (Castor Oil Plant) is a half-hardy annual with large, deep-brown leaves, bright red flower buds and spiny seed pods. It grows 1.5–1.8m/ 5–6ft high.

ZEA MAYS (Sweet Corn) is well known as a vegetable, but there are also ornamental varieties with variegated leaves. They range in height from 90cm/3ft to 1.5m/ 5ft, and are raised as half-hardy annuals.

LUNARIA ANNUA *'Variegata'*, a biennial, grows about 75cm/2¹/₂ ft high and has variegated leaves and crimson flowers. The variety *'Stella'* has creamy white leaves, blotched and splashed with green and white starry flowers.

TRANSPARENTLY HONEST

Lunaria annua *has many names, such as Two-pennies-in-a-purse, Shillings, and Money-in-both-pockets. These all refer to its unusual triple-skinned seed-pods. However, it gained the name Honesty not through their shape, but because the innermost skin is transparent.*

ANNUALS AND BIENNIALS FOR CHALKY SOILS

❖

MOST plants grow best in slightly acid soil. The acidity or alkalinity of soil is measured on the pH scale, ranging from 0 to 14. A pH below 7.0 is acid; above, alkaline or chalky.

Acid soils can be improved by adding lime in the form of hydrated lime or ground limestone. Chalky soils, however, are more difficult to change. Using acid fertilizers, such as sulphate of ammonia, and digging in some well-decomposed manure and compost helps to reduce alkalinity, but if the underlying ground has thick layers of chalk the problem is difficult to resolve. In these conditions, it is best to grow plants that like alkaline soil. Many annuals and biennials grow successfully in these conditions.

TESTING FOR LIME

Discovering if soil is alkaline or acid is easy. At one time, the only way for an amateur to judge the soil's pH was to use a soil-testing kit that involved mixing a soil sample with water, adding chemicals and comparing its colour against a chart which indicated the pH.

Nowadays, a meter with a probe and dial enables readings to be taken quickly and easily. The meter comes with directions, as well as instructions on how to adjust the soil pH. Digital soil pH testers are also available.

These are ideal tools for people who are slightly colour-blind.

COSMOS BIPINNATUS *(Cosmea) is a half-hardy annual, 90cm/3ft high and with white, crimson, pink or rose flowers during mid and late summer. Sow seeds 6mm/¹/₄in deep in 16°C/61°F in late winter or early spring. Plant them 50–60cm/20–24in apart.*

GODETIA GRANDIFLORA *is a hardy annual that flowers during summer. Many varieties, most 30–38cm/12–15in high, both double and single flowered. Sow in late spring, 6mm/¹/₄in deep in drills 23cm/9in apart, where they are to flower.*

LAVATERA TRIMESTRIS *(Mallow) is a hardy annual, 60–90cm/2–3ft high and with rosy pink flowers from mid to late summer. Sow seeds in spring, 12mm/¹/₂in deep in drills 23cm/9in apart, where they are to flower. Thin the seedlings 45–50cm/18–20in apart.*

LYCHNIS VISCARIA *(German Catchfly), a hardy annual, has a wealth of carmine flowers during early and mid-summer on plants 30cm/12in high. Sow seeds in spring, 6mm/¹/4in deep in drills 23cm/9in apart, where they are to flower. Later, thin the seedlings 7.5cm/3in apart.*

NEMESIA STRUMOSA *is a half-hardy annual with flowers in many colours during early summer and into the early part of late summer. They range in height from 20cm/8in to 45cm/18in. Sow seeds 3mm/¹/8in deep in 16°C/61°F in late winter or spring. Plant 10–15cm/ 4–6in apart.*

ZINNIA ELEGANS *(Youth-and-old-age) is a half-hardy annual 60–75cm/2–2¹/2 ft high, although dwarf strains are only 15–30cm/6–12in. Wide colour range. Sow seeds 6mm/¹/4in deep in 16°C/ 61°F during early and mid-spring. Set plants 15–30cm/ 6–12in apart, depending on their height.*

FURTHER PLANTS FOR CHALKY SOILS

- Alcea rosea (Althea rosea) *(Hollyhock) – biennial.*
- Arctotis x hybrida *(African Daisy) – half-hardy annual.*
- Centaurea cyanus *(Cornflower) – hardy annual.*
- Clarkia elegans *– hardy annual.*
- Coreopsis tinctoria *– hardy annual.*
- Delphinium consolida *(Larkspur) – hardy annual.*
- Echium lycopsis *(Purple Viper's Bugloss) – hardy annual.*
- Gysophila elegans *(Baby's Breath) – hardy annual.*
- Iberis umbellata *(Candytuft) – hardy annual.*
- Lathyrus odoratus *(Sweet Pea) – hardy annual.*
- Linaria maroccana *(Toadflax) – hardy annual.*
- Linum grandiflorum 'Rubrum' *(Scarlet Flax) – hardy annual.*
- Lobelia erinus *– half-hardy annual.*
- Lunaria annua *(Honesty) – biennial.*
- Malcolmia maritima *(Virginian Stock) – hardy annual.*
- Nigella damascena *(Love-in-a-mist) – hardy annual.*
- Petunia x hybrida *– half-hardy annual.*
- Phlox drummondii *(Annual Phlox) – half–hardy annual.*
- Rudbeckia hirta *(Black-eyed-Susan) – hardy annual.*
- Salvia splendens *(Scarlet Salvia) – half-hardy annual.*
- Scabiosa atropurpurea *(Sweet Scabious) – hardy annual.*
- Verbena x hybrida *(Vervain) – half-hardy annual.*

POT PLANTS
FOR HOME DECORATION

❖

MANY flowering plants for growing indoors, in greenhouses and conservatories are raised from seeds. Some of these, such as the Fairy Primrose *(Primula malacoides)*, *P. obconica* and *P. sinensis* have a perennial nature, while others, like Persian Violet *(Exacum affine)*, can be grown as either an annual or a biennial.

Although many of these plants grow as perennials if well cared for, they are best treated as temporary houseplants and discarded after their flowers fade.

High temperatures are not needed. Houseplant primulas flower from mid-winter to spring and need only a temperature of 10–13°C/50–55°F. Indeed, too much heat often reduces the length of flowering periods.

INDOOR AND OUTSIDE

Some of these plants, such as the Slipper Flower *(Calceolaria x herbeohybrida)* and Butterfly Flower *(Schizanthus pinnatus)*, can be grown indoors as well as in a garden border or container on a patio. Outdoors, Slipper Flowers behave as a biennial, blooming from early to the latter part of mid-summer from seeds sown during the previous year. To raise Butterfly Flowers that will flower outdoors during summer, sow seeds in early spring and plant in the garden after plants have been acclimatized to outdoor conditions.

Cinerarias *(Senecio cruentus)* flower indoors from early winter to mid-spring. They are also used in windowboxes in mild areas during late winter and spring.

CALCEOLARIA X
HERBEOHYBRIDA *(Slipper Flower)*, 20–45cm/8–18in high, develops masses of pouch-like flowers in shades of red, yellow or orange with attractive spots, from late spring to mid-summer. Sow seeds on the surface of compost a year earlier, in 16°C/61°F.

EXACUM AFFINE *(Persian Violet/German Violet)* has a mass of violet-like flowers from mid-summer to autumn. Each flower has a conspicuous yellow centre. Sow seeds 3mm/1/8in deep from late winter to mid-spring in 18°C/64°F.

CELOSIA ARGENTEA
PLUMOSA *(Prince of Wales' Feather)* develops plume-like, 7.5–15cm/3–6in-long, flower heads on plants 30–60cm/ 12–24in high during mid and late summer. Pink, crimson, amber or yellow flowers. Sow seeds 3mm/1/8in deep in 18°C/64°F from late winter to mid-spring.

CANARY ISLAND FLOWERS

Cinerarias, now known as Senecio cruentus, *have been popular houseplants since being introduced from the Canary Islands towards the latter part of the eighteenth century. They are also used in windowboxes in warm, sheltered areas.*

PRIMULA SINENSIS
(Chinese Primula and also known as P. praenitens) grows 25cm/10in high, with whorls of flowers on stout stems from early winter to early spring. Sow shallowly from late spring to early summer in a cool position. Primula x kewensis *is raised in the same way.*

PRIMULA OBCONICA
grows 23–38cm/9–15in high and produces clustered heads of pink, red, lilac, blue, purple or white flowers from early winter to late spring. Sow seeds 3mm/1/8in deep in 16°C/61°F from late winter to late spring.

PRIMULA MALACOIDES
(Fairy Primrose) grows 20–45cm/8–18in high, with flowers ranging from lilac through red to white from early winter to mid-spring. Some varieties are only 20cm/8in high. Sow seeds thinly from late spring to mid-summer.

SCHIZANTHUS
PINNATUS *(Butterfly Flower/Poor Man's Orchid) grows 45cm–1.2m/1 1/2–4ft high, although it is the short types at 30–45cm/1–1 1/2 ft that are best as houseplants. They flower in spring indoors, with seeds sown 3mm/1/8in deep in 16°C/ 61°F during mid-summer.*

SENECIO CRUENTUS
(Cineraria cruenta) grows 25–45cm/10–18in high and develops dome-shaped clusters of white, mauve, blue, pink or red flowers from early winter to mid-spring. Sow seeds 3mm/ 1/8in deep in 13°C/55°F from spring to mid-summer.

ANNUAL CLIMBERS

❖

MANY climbers can be easily raised from seeds. Some are hardy enough to be sown outdoors in the positions in which they will flower, others need the comfort of gentle warmth in late winter or spring to give them a start in life. Subsequently, they are planted out into their growing and flowering positions.

A few of these plants, such as the Cup-and-saucer Plant *(Cobaea scandens)*, grow as perennials and can also be grown in greenhouses and conservatories, where they attain slightly larger proportions than when outdoors.

All of the climbers listed here are ideal for bringing colour to walls and fences, but provide a supporting framework when growing them against walls. The soil at the base of a wall dries out rapidly, so water plants regularly.

FURTHER CLIMBERS

• **Lathyrus chlorantha** *'Lemonade'* grows 1.5–2.4m/ 5–8ft high and develops sweet pea-like, green coloured flowers from mid to late summer.
• **Lathyrus odoratus** *(Sweet Pea)* – pages 50–51.
• **Mina lobata** (Quamoclit lobata) grows 1.2–1.8m/ 4–6ft high and produces several hundred stems bearing rich red flowers that mature through orange to yellow and finally white. Grow it as a half-hardy annual.
• **Rhodochiton atrosanguineum** *(Purple Bell Vine)* creates a mass of parasol-shaped, blackish-purple to crimson flowers during summer and into autumn.

ASARINA SCANDENS
'Jewel Mixed' (Climbing Snapdragon) develops violet, white, pink and deep blue flowers about four months after sowing. Sow seeds in gentle warmth in mid-spring and set the plants 10cm/4in apart. It grows 1.2–2.4m/ 4–8ft high.

CAJOPHORA
(CAIOPHORA) LATERITA
'Frothy' has 5cm/2in-wide flowers that change from coppery-orange to white. Sow seeds in gentle warmth in mid-spring and set the plants 10cm/4in apart in groups of four or five. It grows 1.2–1.8m/4–6ft high.

COBAEA SCANDENS
(Cup-and-saucer Plant/Cathedral Bells) develops purple, bell-shaped flowers about 6.5cm/2½in long during summer. Sow seeds in gentle warmth in early or mid-spring and plant 45cm/18in apart. It grows 3–6m/10–20ft high.

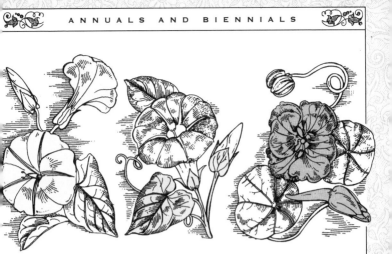

CONVOLVULUS MAJOR (Ipomoea purpurea/Pharbitis purpurea) *is a vigorous climber with funnel-shaped, purple flowers from mid to late summer. Sow seeds in spring, where plants will flower, 12mm/ ^{1}/2 in deep, 30cm/12in apart. Plants grow to 2.4–3m/8–10ft and soon cover supports.*

IPOMOEA TRICOLOR 'Heavenly Blue' (I. rubro-caerulea/I. violacea/Pharbitis tricolor) *is the well-known Morning Glory and dislays red-purple to blue flowers from mid to late summer. Sow seeds in gentle warmth in mid-spring and set young plants 30cm/12in apart. Plants grow about 2.4m/8ft high.*

TROPAEOLUM MAJUS 'Climbing Mixed' (Nasturtium) *creates a wealth of cerise, scarlet, orange, yellow or cream flowers from early to late summer. Sow seeds in spring, where they are to flower and thin the seedlings 25–38cm/10–15in apart. Plants grow 1.8–2.4m/6–8ft high.*

ECCREMOCARPUS SCABER 'Anglia Hybrids Mixed' (Chilean Glory Flower). *Sow seeds in gentle warmth in early spring and put the plants outside as soon as all risk of frost has passed, setting them 45cm/18in apart. Plants grow 1.8–3m/6–10ft high.*

LATHYRUS LATIFOLIUS (Everlasting Sweet Pea) *has a perennial nature with flowers from early to late summer. Sow seeds 12mm/ ^{1}/2 in deep in spring, where they are to flower. Thin the seedlings 38–45cm/15–18in apart. Plants grow 2.4–3m/8–10ft high.*

TROPAEOLUM PEREGRINUM (Canary Creeper) *produces irregularly shaped, yellow flowers from mid-summer to autumn. Sow seeds in gentle warmth in spring and set plants 75cm/ 2 ^{1}/2 ft apart, or sow in position in late spring. Plants grow 1.8–3m/6–10ft high.*

ANNUALS FOR
ROCK GARDENS

❖

BOTH hardy and half-hardy annuals are useful in rock gardens, inexpensively filling in gaps while more permanent plants are being established. They create colour in summer and therefore are useful additions to the mainly spring and early-summer flowering nature of most alpine and rock garden plants.

In large rock gardens they are often used to create colour drifts that help to unify the entire area. Some, such as *Portulaca grandiflora*, create dense ground cover.

The half-hardy annuals are raised in gentle warmth in spring and put into their flowering positions when the risk of frost has passed. Hardy annuals, however, are sown where they flower. Fork the soil, lightly firm it and then thinly and evenly scatter the seeds. Sieve soil over them and gently firm the surface. If birds are a nuisance, place twiggy sticks on the surface. When the seedlings are large enough to handle, thin them out. Re-firm soil around those that remain.

SELF-SOWN SEEDLINGS

Most annuals freely scatter their seeds at the end of summer. This is not usually a problem, but in rock gardens, where space is often limited and, perhaps, annuals are only temporary occupants, it may create problems during the following year. Therefore, as soon as their display is over, pull them up. The hardy annual types are the ones that are most likely to re-seed themselves, although half-hardy types are likely to act similarly in warm areas.

ANAGALLIS LINIFOLIA *'Gentian Blue' (Scarlet Pimpernel), grown as a half-hardy annual, reaches 15– 23cm/6–9in high and bears blue flowers from early to late summer. Sow seeds in 16°C/61°F in early spring and plant 25–30cm/ 10–12in apart.*

ADONIS AESTIVALIS *(Pheasant's Eye), a hardy annual, grows 25–30cm/ 10–12in high and displays deep crimson flowers with black centres from early to late summer. Sow seeds 6mm/¹⁄₄in deep in spring, where they are to flower. Later, thin the seedlings 23cm/9in apart.*

FELICIA BERGERIANA *(Kingfisher Daisy) is a half-hardy annual, growing 15cm/6in high and bearing steel-blue flowers with yellow centres from early to late summer. Sow seeds in 16°C/61°F in early spring and plant 15cm/6in apart. Plant in full sun and a well-drained soil.*

IONOPSIDIUM ACAULE *(Violet Cress) is a hardy annual, 5–7.5cm/2–3in high and with four–petalled, mauve or white flowers, tinged with purple, from early to late summer. Sow seeds 6mm/1/4in deep in spring where they are to flower. Thin the seedlings 5–7.5cm/ 2–3in apart.*

LIMNANTHES DOUGLASII *(Poached Egg Plant) is a hardy annual, 15cm/6in high, with yellow-centred white flowers from early to mid-summer. Sow seeds 3mm/1/8in deep during spring in their flowering positions. Later, thin the seedlings 10cm/ 4in apart.*

URSINIA ANETHOIDES *is a half-hardy annual, growing 23cm/9in high and bearing orange, daisy-like flowers with purple centres from early to late summer. Sow seeds 3mm/1/8in deep in 15°C/59°F during early spring. Set the plants in small groups 25–30cm/ 10–12in apart.*

MESEMBRYANTHEMUM CRINIFLORUM *(Livingstone Daisy), grown as a half-hardy annual, is 10–15cm/4–6in high and displays daisy-like, pink, crimson, orange, rose and apricot flowers from early to late summer. Sow seeds 3mm/1/8in deep in 15°C/59°F in early spring. Set the young plants 30cm/12in apart.*

FURTHER ANNUALS

- Antirrhinum majus – *dwarf forms – half-hardy annual.*
- Eschscholzia caespitosa – *hardy annual.*
- Gazania x hybrida – *half-hardy annual.*
- Gilia lutea – *hardy annual.*
- Godetia – *dwarf forms – hardy annual.*

- Nemophila menziesii – *hardy annual.*
- Phacelia campanularia – *hardy annual.*
- Platystemon californicus – *hardy annual.*
- Portulaca grandiflora *(Sun Plant) – half-hardy annual; ideal for covering large areas.*

FRAGRANT
ANNUALS AND BIENNIALS

❖

RAGRANCE is often considered to be an indication of a civilized garden. Dramatic splashes of colour are always attractive, but when combined with a pleasurable scent they are even more desirable. This combination is easily achieved by sowing or planting annuals and biennials.

There are many plants to choose from and some, such as *Matthiola bicornis*, introduce scent to evenings and nights. A superb and fragrant combination is the Night–scented Stock *(Matthiola bicornis)* and the Virginian Stock *(Malcolmia maritima)*. Plant these together under a window: the straggly and sprawling nature of the Night–scented Stock is tempered by the shorter and tidier Virginian Stock.

OTHER
SCENTED PLANTS

• Centaurea moschata *(Sweet Sultan) – hardy annual.*
• Dianthus barbatus *(Sweet William) – biennial.*
• Heliotropium x hybridum *(Cherry Pie) – half-hardy annual.*
• Hesperis matronalis *(Sweet Rocket) – biennial.*
• Limnanthes douglassi *(Poached Egg Plant) – hardy annual.*
• Matthiola bicornis *(Night-scented Stock) – hardy annual.*
• Mirabilis jalapa *(Four o'Clock Plant/Marvel of Peru) – half-hardy annual.*
• Nicotiana alata *(Tobacco Plant) – half-hardy annual.*

ALYSSUM MARITIMUM *(Sweet Alyssum), now known as* Lobularia maritima, *develops flowers with a bouquet resembling new-mown hay. There are several flower colours, including white, shades of purple, pink and rose. It is a hardy annual usually grown as a half-hardy annual.*

WALLFLOWERS (Cheiranthus *and* Erysimum *species) are mostly sweetly scented. By nature they are perennial but invariably grown as biennials. Growing them in combination with tulips helps to extend the period of colour. Heights range from 15cm/6in to 45cm/18in.*

DIANTHUS BARBATUS *(Sweet William) is a cottage-garden flower with a sweet fragrance. Although a perennial plant, it is always grown as a biennial, when it flowers during early and mid-summer. Plants are 20–60cm/8–24in high, and are best planted 20–25cm/8–10in apart.*

LATHYRUS ODORATUS *(Sweet Pea) is a sweetly scented, hardy annual climber. Some grow 3m/ 10ft high, others only 45cm/ 1½ ft. They flower from early to late summer.*

NICOTIANA x SANDERAE *(Flowering Tobacco Plant) is well known for its sweetly scented flowers, which appear from early to late summer. It is a half-hardy annual.*

MALCOLMIA MARITIMA *(Virginian Stock), a sweetly scented hardy annual, flowers for about eight weeks, four weeks after being sown.*

RESEDA ODORATA *(Mignonette) is a hardy annual, sweetly scented and attractive to bees. Sow seeds in spring, where they are to flower. Flowers appear from early summer to autumn.*

VERBENA x HYBRIDA *(Vervain) is a half-hardy annual with primrose-like, fragrant flowers borne in clustered heads from early summer to autumn. Verbena rigida also has fragrant flowers.*

MATTHIOLA INCANA *'Apple Blossom' (Stocks) can be grown as a half-hardy annual. It has clove-scented flowers and grows 30cm/ 12in high. 'Legacy', 30– 38cm/ 12–15in high, is another superbly scented stock.*

THE GOOD PLANT

The name Verbena is thought to be derived from Herbena, meaning the good plant. This is because Vervain (Verbena officinalis) was widely used by early man, and featured in pagan religious practices.

ANNUALS FOR HANGING BASKETS

HALF-HARDY annuals are ideal plants for drenching hanging baskets with colour throughout summer. Seeds are sown in gentle warmth in greenhouses in late winter or early spring, pricked out and the young plants slowly accustomed to outdoor conditions. It is at this stage that they are vulnerable to damage from frost. Ideally, plant them into hanging baskets and place in a greenhouse or conservatory until all risk of frost has passed. This gives them time to become established before being put outside. Should an unexpected frost be forecast after they have been put outdoors, place a couple of sheets of newspaper over them, removing them late the following morning, when the temperature has risen.

ASARINA PURPUSII *'Victoria Falls'* is grown as a half-hardy annual, when it creates a mass of tumbling, cerise-purple trumpets from early summer to autumn. The stems trail for about 30cm/12in. Sow seeds on the surface of compost in mid-spring and place in 20–24°C/70–75°F.

LOBELIA ERINUS *'Cascade Mixed'* is a half-hardy annual with a trailing nature. Throughout summer it displays carmine, maroon, pink, violet and white flowers. Sow seeds on the surface of compost in early spring, placing them in 16°C/16°F. Prick out the seedlings in small clusters.

CAMPANULA CARPATICA *'Bellissimo'* is a perennial, but invariably raised as a half-hardy annual. It develops blue or white, trumpet-shaped flowers throughout summer. During spring, sow seeds by just lightly pressing them into the compost. Place in gentle warmth.

IMPATIENS *'Mega Orange'* is grown as a half-hardy annual, when it creates a feast of red flowers with white stripes throughout summer – whatever the weather. Sow seeds 3mm/ 1/8in deep in 16°C/61°F during early spring. Ensure the plants are not damaged by frost.

TROPAEOLUM MAJUS
'Peach Melba' is a trailing
nasturtium. Although
normally a hardy annual,
when grown for flowering in
containers it is best sown
3–6mm/¹/8–¹/4in deep in
mid-spring in small pots.
Place in gentle warmth;
lower the temperature after
the seeds germinate.

NEMOPHILA MACULATA
'Five-Spot' develops pale blue
flowers with deep blue spots
at the edge of each petal.
Normally, it is a hardy
annual, but when grown in
containers is sown 6mm/¹/4in
deep in small pots in spring
and placed in gentle warmth.
After germination, start to
lower the temperature.

NEMOPHILA MENZIESII
'Pennie Black' develops
masses of slightly bell-shaped,
silvery white edged flowers
from early to late summer.
The edges of the flowers are
scalloped. It grows equally
well in full sun and shade.
Raise new plants in the same
way as recommended for
Nemophila maculata.

PANSY 'Water Colours Mixed' develops
masses of flowers whatever the weather.
It can be grow to flower in winter and
spring, as well as summer. For summer
displays, sow seeds 6mm/ ¹/4in deep in
10–15°C/ 50–59°F in late winter or
early spring. Prick out the seedlings into
seed-trays and acclimatize them slowly to
outdoor conditions.

PETUNIA x HYBRIDA 'Super Cascade
Improved Mixed' is grown as a half-
hardy annual. Throughout summer it
bears white, pink, blush, blue, cerise,
salmon and scarlet flowers on cascading
stems. Sow seeds on the surface of
compost in early spring and place in
15°C/ 59°F. Slowly acclimatize the
plants to outdoor conditions.

ANNUALS FOR CUT FLOWERS

GROWING bright, attractive flowers that can be cut and displayed indoors in vases is a bonus with many hardy and half-hardy annuals.

To ensure that the flowers last a long time indoors, cut them in the morning while their leaves and stems are full of moisture. When severing the stems, use a sharp knife or scissors and cut at a 45-degree angle. Then remove the lower leaves and place them in buckets of deep, clean water in a cool, shaded room. During the morning, carefully arrange the flowers in vases.

Once arranged, check them every day, removing faded flowers and topping up with fresh water. Proprietary additives can be mixed with the water to extend the flowers' lives.

OTHER PLANTS

- Amaranthus caudatus (Love-lies-bleeding) – hardy annual.
- Antirrhinum majus (Snapdragon) – half-hardy annual.
- Coreopsis tinctoria (Tickseed) – hardy annual.
- Cosmos bipinnatus (Cosmea) – half-hardy annual.
- Lathyrus odoratus (Sweet Pea) – hardy annual.
- Reseda odorata (Mignonette) – hardy annual.
- Schizanthus pannatus (Butterfly Flower/Poor Man's Orchid) – half-hardy annual.
- Verbena x hybrida (Vervain) – half-hardy annual.

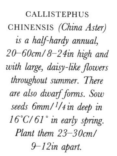

CALLISTEPHUS CHINENSIS (China Aster) is a half-hardy annual, 20–60cm/8–24in high and with large, daisy-like flowers throughout summer. There are also dwarf forms. Sow seeds 6mm/1/4in deep in 16°C/61° in early spring. Plant them 23–30cm/ 9–12in apart.

CALENDULA OFFICINALIS (Pot Marigold) is a hardy annual, 30–60cm/1–2ft high and with yellow or orange flowers throughout summer. Sow seeds 12mm/1/2in deep in drills 23cm/9in apart in spring, in position. Thin seedlings 30cm/12in apart.

DELPHINIUM CONSOLIDA (Larkspur) is a hardy annual, 90cm– 1.2m/3–4ft high, with spires of pink, red, purple or white flowers from early to mid-summer. In spring, sow seeds 6mm/1/4in deep, where they are to flower. Later, thin the seedlings 23cm/9in apart.

GAILLARDIA PULCHELLA *(Blanket Flower) is a half-hardy annual, about 30–45cm/12–18in high, with large, daisy-like flowers from mid-summer to the frosts of autumn. Sow seeds 6mm/1/4in deep in 15°C/59°F during spring. Set the plants 25cm/10in apart.*

BLANKET FLOWER

Gaillardia puchella *probably gained its common name from its colourful flowers that resemble the bright, zigzag-patterned blankets of the North American Indians.*

GYPSOPHILA ELEGANS *(Baby's Breath) is a hardy annual, 50–60cm/20–24in high, with clouds of white, pink or rose-coloured flowers throughout summer. Sow seeds where they are to flower, 6mm/1/4in deep and in drills 23cm/9in apart during spring. Thin the seedlings 25–30cm/10–12in apart.*

IBERIS UMBELLATA *(Candytuft/Globe Candytuft) is a hardy annual, 15–38cm/6–15in high, with domed heads of red, purple or white flowers from early to late summer. Sow seeds where they are to flower, 6mm/1/4in deep in drills 23cm/9in apart during early and mid-spring. Thin the seedlings 23cm/9in apart.*

GODETIA
GRANDIFLORA, *a hardy annual, grows 30–38cm/12–15in high and bears single, double or semi-double flowers in pink, white, cherry-red or salmon during mid and late summer. Sow seeds where the plants are to flower, 6mm/1/4in deep and in drills 23cm/9in apart, in late spring. Thin the seedlings 15cm/6in apart.*

NIGELLA DAMASCENA *(Love-in-a-mist), a hardy annual and 45–60cm/11/2–2ft high, has finely cut leaves and blue or white flowers from early to mid-summer. Sow seeds where the plants are to flower, 6mm/1/4in deep and in drills 23cm/9in apart during spring. Subsequently, thin the seedlings 15–23cm/6–9in apart.*

EVERLASTING FLOWERS

❖

HESE are well worth growing as they brighten both gardens and homes, and they are very easily dried.

As soon as the flowers first open, cut them with long stems. Do not wait for the flowers to age before cutting them. Tie into small bunches and hang them upside down in a room that is dry and well-ventilated.

Some of these everlasting flowers can be sown where they are to flower, but most are grown as half-hardy plants: raised in gentle warmth in spring and later planted into a garden. Always choose a warm, sunny, position for them, that is sheltered from the wind.

IMMORTELLE

The everlasting Australian flower Helichrysum bracteatum *gained the name Immortelle – shortened from Fleur Immortelle – from its use in funeral wreaths in the south of France. Although a perennial in Australia, in countries with temperate climates it is grown as a half-hardy annual. In North America it is more widely known as Strawflower.*

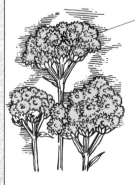

CELOSIA *'Flamingo Feather' is a half-hardy annual, 60–75cm/2–2¹/₂ft high. During summer it bears rose and deep pink, 10–13cm/4 5in-long, unusually shaped flower heads.*

CRASPEDIA GLOBOSA *'Drumstick' is usually grown as a half-hardy annual, and reaches 60–90cm/2–3ft high. It has silver leaves and yellow flowers.*

GNAPHALIUM *'Fairy Gold', usually grown as a half-hardy annual, is 30cm/12in high. It develops silvery grey leaves and double, yellow to orange flowers.*

GOMPHRENA HYBRIDA *'Full Mix' is a half-hardy annual, 45–60cm/1¹/₂–2ft tall and with a wide range of colourful flowers from mid-summer to autumn.*

HELICHRYSUM
'Bright Bikini Mixed'
(Strawflower) grows 38cm/
15in high and is a half-
hardy annual. From mid-
summer to autumn it reveals
large, daisy-like flowers in
about eight different colours.
'Pastel Mixed' is taller, at
90cm–1.2m/3–4ft.

HELIPTERUM ROSEUM
GRANDIFLORUM *'Double*
Mixed' is a half-hardy
annual, 38–45cm/15–18in
high and with large flowers
in shades of pink, yellow and
white during mid and late
summer. The colours are
retained long after the flowers
are cut and dried.

LIMONIUM SINUATUM
'Azure' (Sea Lavender) is
grown as a half-hardy
annual, 45–60cm/1^1/$_2$–2ft
high. This variety develops
blue flowers from mid-
summer to autumn, but there
are many others, in colours
including yellow, orange,
pink, white and carmine.

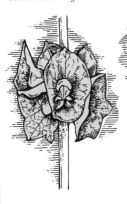

SCABIOSA STELLATA
'Drumstick' is a hardy
annual about 30cm/12in
high and with up to thirty
stems bearing blue flowers
which change to burnished
bronze. The round,
drumstick-like heads will
introduce an attractive and
unusual dimension to dried
flower arrangements.

MOLUCCELLA LAEVIS
(Bells of Ireland) is a half-
hardy annual that grows
60–75cm/2–2^1/$_2$ft high.
Throughout summer it has
tall stems packed with olive
to emerald green bells. When
cut, they last for several
years. It is ideal for
introducing height to dried
flower arrangements. It is
also a superb plant in fresh
flower displays.

AMERICAN VARIATION

Whereas in Europe it is **Helichrysum**
bracteatum *that is known as Immortelle, in*
North America it is the southern European
Xeranthemum annum. *This plant is grown*
as a hardy annual and develops large, daisy-
like, white, pink, rose and lilac-coloured flowers
on plants 45–60cm/1^1/$_2$–2ft tall during early
and mid-summer.

Both of these plants demand a sunny,
sheltered position and light, well-drained soil.

PESTS AND DISEASES

❖

WHEN plants are grown in large groups, they create a ready source of food for pests. These include those that live in soil and those that suck sap from leaves. Even birds can be a problem, delighting in disturbing newly sown seeds, nipping off flower buds and leaves.

Some of these problems can be avoided by digging soil deeply in winter and picking out grubs, or leaving them exposed for birds or frost to deal with. Additionally, avoid planting half-hardy annuals too close together, or not thinning hardy ones far enough apart – both of which cause congestion.

Another preventative measure is to pull up all plants in autumn, as soon as their display is over. Either place them on a compost heap or, if infected with diseases, burn them. Also, pull up or hoe off weeds during summer, as they may harbour diseases and pests.

APHIDS *(greenfly) are the main pests of plants. They suck sap, causing mottling and distortion of shoots, leaves and flowers. Spray with a proprietary insecticide regularly throughout summer.*

BIRDS *often disturb newly sown seeds, and tear young shoots and leaves. Place twiggy sticks over the surface, or stretch black cotton between sticks. Remove this protection later when plants are established.*

BOTRYTIS *(grey mould) forms a fluffy mould on leaves, stems and flowers, especially where damp, cool, airless conditions prevail. Avoid congestion and spray with a fungicide throughout the summer.*

CATERPILLARS *chew leaves and flowers, eventually completely destroying plants. Pick off and remove these pests. Alternatively, use an insecticide. Pull up and burn seriously infected plants.*

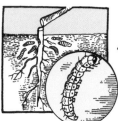

CUTWORMS *are the larvae of certain moths. They live in the topsoil and chew the stems of seedlings, causing them to collapse. Dust the soil with a gamma-HCH and remove all weeds. Dig the soil thoroughly in winter.*

DAMPING OFF *causes seedlings in seed-trays to collapse and die, due to overcrowding, high temperatures and excessively moist compost. Attacks can be prevented by using a proprietary fungicide.*

EARWIGS *chew flowers, soft leaves and stems, especially at night. Pick off and destroy these pests or trap them in pots of straw inverted on canes. Alternatively, dust with gamma-HCH.*

FROGHOPPERS *create masses of froth, widely known as cuckoo-spit, usually in leaf joints. They pierce soft stems and leaves and suck sap, causing distortion. Spray them with an insecticide.*

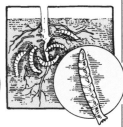

LEATHERJACKETS *are the larvae of craneflies and live in soil, chewing roots and causing plants to wilt. They are a particular problem in newly dug grass land. Dust affected soil with an insecticide.*

POWDERY MILDEW *forms a white, powdery coating on leaves, stems and flowers. It is encouraged by congestion, lack of air circulation, and dry soil. Use a fungicide.*

MILLIPEDES *chew stems and roots and are especially troublesome in damp soil to which organic material has been added. Dust the soil with gamma-HCH and dig it deeply in winter.*

RUST *is especially a problem with Hollyhocks and Mallows (Lavatera). Rusts are difficult to control and therefore it is best to pull up and burn infected plants. Also, remove weeds.*

SLUGS *are especially troublesome during wet and warm weather, when they chew all parts of plants. They feed at night and therefore are not always seen. Use slug baits or remove and destroy.*

SNAILS *are, like slugs, pests of the night and especially damaging during warm, wet weather. They chew and tear leaves and stems. Pick off and destroy as soon as they are seen. Also, use baits.*

WIREWORMS *are the larvae of clickbeetles. They inhabit soil, chewing roots and causing the death of plants. They are especially troublesome on newly dug grassland. Dust the soil with gamma-HCH.*

ANNUAL AND BIENNIAL CALENDAR

❖

SPRING

This is the main time to raise plants from seeds, although late winter and early summer are also ideal for some of them. Half-hardy annuals are sown in greenhouses during late winter and early spring; hardy annuals are sown outdoors in late spring and early summer; while biennials are sown outdoors in seed-beds in late spring and early summer.

IN THE GREENHOUSE

- Sow seeds of half-hardy annuals in gentle warmth in late winter or early spring (14–15).
- Prick off seedlings of half-hardy annuals into seed-trays to prevent them becoming congested and diseased (18–19).
- Slowly harden off half-hardy bedding plants, so that they become used to outdoor conditions (22–23).
- In late spring, pot up half-hardy annuals grown for indoor decoration (20–21).
- In spring, make more space for plants by constructing shelves suspended from the glazing bars in the greenhouse (20–21).

IN THE GARDEN

- Rake the soil where hardy annuals are to be sown, then shuffle sideways in 23cm/9in-wide strips over the surface. Lightly rake the soil surface in preparation for sowing seeds in late spring (12–13).
- Sow hardy-annual seeds in late spring in mild areas (12–13).
- Protect newly sown hardy annuals seeds from disturbance by birds (12–13).
- Sow seeds of biennials in late spring or early summer (16–17).

SUMMER

Early summer is when gardens are suddenly ablaze with hardy and half-hardy flowers.

IN THE GREENHOUSE

- In cold areas, where late frosts are possible in early summer, use a greenhouse to provide protection at night (22–23).
- In early summer, prick off seedlings of half-hardy annuals that were sown during late spring (18–19).

IN THE GARDEN

- Sow seeds of hardy annuals in early summer (12–13).
- Protect newly sown hardy annuals from birds (12–13).
- In early summer, sow seeds of biennials in well-prepared seed-beds (16–17).
- Plant established and hardened-off half-hardy annuals into gardens, as soon as all risk of frost has passed (22–23).
- Keep seed-beds of biennial plants free from weeds (25).
- Remove weeds from between rows of hardy annuals. Re-firm the young seedlings (24).
- Thin out hardy annuals (24).
- Thin out or transplant seedlings of biennials (25).
- At the end of summer or during early autumn, transplant biennials to their flowering positions (25). In exceptionally cold areas, this job is left until early spring.
- Plant half-hardy annuals in containers on patios as soon as all risk of damaging frost has passed (22–23).
- Remove dead flowers to encourage the development of further blooms (24).

AUTUMN

This is a time for pulling up and removing half-hardy and hardy annuals which have finished flowering. If left, they create eyesores and encourage attack by harmful pests and diseases.

As soon as seed catalogues become available, send in your order for the seeds you want for the following year. Orders that are left until late winter may not be filled and end in disappointment. In most seed catalogues, seedsmen highlight new varieties and these are always worth trying. Although new to you, they will have been well tested beforehand.

Some gardeners like to collect their own seeds from existing plants, but when F.1 hybrid plants are being grown this is not recommended, as the offspring will not resemble their parents. F.1 plants have greater vigour than ordinary seeds, as well as being more uniform in height and the size of their flowers.

IN THE GARDEN

- Some hardy annuals can be sown in late summer or autumn, as well as in late spring and early summer. This enables larger and earlier-flowering plants to be produced (62).
- In late summer or early autumn, move biennials to their flowering positions (25). If they are planted with tulips or hyacinths, space out the plants and bulbs on the surface before planting them. Alternatively, plant the biennials first, and then put bulbs between them. Annuals and biennials are ideal for planting in new gardens which have yet to be planned in detail: they fill in borders and create colour while you make up your mind about permanent plants such as trees and shrubs.

WINTER

Until seed sowing begins in greenhouses in late winter, this is not a very active period for half-hardy annuals. However, prepare greenhouses in early or mid-winter by scrubbing both the outside and inside to ensure it is free from pests and diseases. Cleaning the glass ensures that the maximum amount of light reaches the seedlings in winter.

Check that heaters are fully operational and that propagation units maintain an even temperature; both electric and paraffin types are available. If the greenhouse is in an exposed position, reduce heating costs by fitting bubble glazing to the inside. And check that the door and ventilators fit their frames and do not allow draughts to enter.

Engage a qualified electrician to examine and test all the electrical circuits and equipment in your garden and greenhouse.

IN THE GREENHOUSE

- Sow seeds of half-hardy annuals in late winter or during early spring (14–15).
- Suitable temperatures to encourage half–hardy seeds to germinate are indicated on pages 26–29.

IN THE GARDEN

- Prepare flower borders, either single or double digging them (10–11). Ensure all perennial weeds are removed.
- Dig and prepare seed-beds in preparation for sowing biennials in late spring and during early summer (16–17).
- During late winter or early spring, re-firm young biennial plants that were planted in late summer or early autumn and have had their roots loosened by frost (25).

USEFUL ANNUAL
AND BIENNIAL TERMS

❖

ANNUAL: *A plant which grows from seed, develops flowers and produces seeds during the same year.*

AUTUMN SOWING: *A few annuals can be sown in autumn for flowering during late spring and early summer of the following year. These include* Antirrhinum majus *(26),* Calendula officinalis *(9, 54),* Iberis umbellata *(33, 55),* Clarkia elegans *(31),* Clarkia pulchella *(31),* Centaurea cyanus *(31),* Eschscholzia californica *(32),* Godetia grandiflora *(42, 55),* Delphinium consolida *(54),* Limnanthes douglasii *(49),* Nigella damascena *(34, 55),* Papaver rhoeas *(35),* Papaver somniferum *(35),* Scabious atropurpurea *(35) and* Lathyrus odoratus *(51).*

BEDDING PLANTS: *Usually refers to half-hardy annuals (some naturally have a perennial nature) that are raised in gentle warmth in late winter or early spring and later planted into gardens to create displays in summer. Biennials are normally planted in late summer or early autumn to create displays during spring or early summer of the following year.*

BIENNIAL: *A plant which has its life cycle spread over two years. During the first year it is raised from seeds and the plants become established. In the second year, it bears flowers and produces seeds.*

COMPOST: *This has two meanings. The first is decomposed vegetable material that is either spread on the surface of soil to form a mulch or dug in during winter. The other meaning is a mixture of loam, sand and peat in which seeds can be sown. Seedlings are also transferred into it, as well as plants. There are also peat-based composts and environmentally-friendly types (see page 19).*

CROCK: *A piece of broken clay pot which is put over a drainage hole in the base of a clay pot. Plastic pots do not need to be crocked.*

CULTIVAR: *A variation of a species or hybrid which has arisen in cultivation. It is indicated by placing single quotation marks around it.*

DOT PLANT: *A plant, usually tall but may also be dominant in terms of colour and shape, that is used to introduce variation and interest in a bedding scheme.*

DOUBLE DIGGING: *This is when the soil is dug to the depth of two spade blades. However, while doing this the soil from the upper level is not mixed with that from the lower one. Compost and manure can be added at the same time and mixed in.*

DRAWN: *Plants or seedlings that are drawn upwards because they have been placed too close together. For this reason, seedlings are pricked out as soon as they can be handled without causing them damage.*

DRILL: *A shallow depression, usually formed with a draw hoe, in which seeds are sown. In the open ground these are usually 6–12mm/^{1}/$_4$–^{1}/$_2$in deep and about 23cm/9in apart.*

F1. HYBRID: *A plant raised from crossing two distinctive and unrelated plants. Such plants have additional vigour.*

FLORE-PLENA: *Used to describe flowers with a larger than normal number of petals. They are described as semi-double or double.*

FLOWER: *The reproductive part of a plant. It is often highly coloured to attract insects; alternatively, it may be scented.*

FRIABLE: *Soil which is crumbly and can be raked to form a tilth.*

GENUS: *A division within a family of plants.*

GERMINATION: *The first step in the development of a seed into a plant.*

HALF-HARDY ANNUAL: *These are plants that are raised in gentle warmth in late winter or early spring and planted into gardens when all risk of frost has passed. Many have a perennial nature in their native countries.*

HARDEN OFF: *Slowly acclimatizing half-hardy annuals to typical outdoor temperatures before they are planted outdoors into flower beds or containers.*

HYBRID: *A plant whose parents come from two distinct and different species. This is indicated by placing an x between the generic and specific names. An example of this is Viola x wittrockiana.*

INFLORESCENCE: *The part of a plant that bears single or clustered flowers.*

LOAM: *Friable topsoil, neither excessively sandy nor clayey, which is used to form soil-based compost in which seeds can be sown or seedlings and plants grown.*

NEUTRAL: *Soil that is neither acid nor alkaline. It has a pH value of 7.0. Most plants grow well in slightly acid soil, with a pH value of 6.5.*

NURSERYBED: *An area into which young plants are transplanted before being planted into a garden.*

PH: *A method of measuring the acidity or alkalinity of soil. It is indicated on a pH scale from 0 to 14. A reading of pH 7.0 is neutral, while figures below indicate increasing acidity and, above, greater alkalinity.*

POTTING: *Transferring a plant from a seed-tray into a pot. This gives the plant more space in which to develop and grow. It also provides each plant with more compost and food.*

PRICKING OFF: *Transferring seedlings from pots or seed-trays in which they germiminated into seed-trays or pots so that each of them has more space.*

PRICKING OUT: *see* PRICKING OFF.

SEED-BED: *A piece of soil, evenly dug and firmed so that seeds can be sown in it. This is done in shallow drills, about 23cm/9in apart. The ensuing seedlings are either thinned or transplanted to a nurserybed until large enough to be planted into a garden.*

SEEDLING: *A young plant after germination. It has a single, unbranched stem. When the seedling is being pricked out into wider spacings, the delicate stem must not be crushed: hold the seedling by one of its leaves instead of the stem.*

SINGLE DIGGING: *Turning over the soil to the depth of a spade's blade, about 25cm/10in deep. This is performed in winter in preparation for planting or sowing seeds. All perennial weeds are removed and burned. If left, they will grow again during the following year.*

SPECIES: *A sub-division of a genus.*

SPIT: *The depth of a spade's blade.*

STOPPING: *The removal of the tip of a shoot to encourage the development of sideshoots. It also encourages seedlings to become firmer and less susceptible to diseases and damage.*

THINNING: *The process of removing surplus seedlings, so that the remaining ones have more space in which to develop. Sometimes this is performed in two stages; the first thinning to half the desired spacing, and later to the full distance. Re-firm the soil around all the seedlings that remain.*

TILTH: *Loose, friable surface soil. This is essential when sowing hardy annuals and biennials in seed-beds outdoors.*

TRANSPIRATION: *The continual loss of moisture from the surfaces of leaves and stems. The temperature and wind strongly influence the rate by which water leaves a plant.*

TRANSPLANTING: *Moving young plants from seed-trays or a nurserybed into their flowering positions. Ensure that their roots are covered with soil, gently but firmly spread over them.*

VARIEGATED: *A leaf that is regularly or irregularly marked in a different colour. Annuals and biennials which are variegated are used to create colour and interest throughout summer.*

VARIETY: *A variant within a species which has arisen in the wild, rather than in cultivation. It is indicated by placing single quotation marks around it.*

VENTILATION: *The flow of air through a greenhouse or cold frame. It is created by opening ventilators and doors,or in garden frames by propping up one side. Avoid draughts blowing on plants.*

WEED: *Any plant that is growing where it is not required. Clearly, it mostly applies to native plants that grow between and around cultivated and desired types. Remove weeds at the earliest opportunity, as they steal moisture and nutrients from cultivated plants, cause congestion, encourage pests and diseases, and their later removal will disturb the soil.*

INDEX